Rasdu Atoll

Veligandu

● Rasdu
②

Kuramathi
Kuramathi

① Gangehi

Ukulhas

Mathiveri
●
Nika Hotel
(Kuda Folhudhu)

Avi Island
(Velidhoo)

③

■ Madoogali

Maayaafushi

Feridhu

Bathala

Halaveli
④

Fesdu ⑥

⑤

Ellaidoo

ARI ATOLL
(ALIF ATOLL)

Malhos

⑦

Himandhu

Athurugau

Moofushi

Hanya Midhu

Thundu-
fushi

Omadhu

Kuburudhu

Mahibadhu

Mandhu

Rangali
Finolhu

Angaagau

Twin Island
(Maafushivaru)

Ranveli Beach Resort
(Villingilivaru)

Mirihi

Dhagethi

Angels Beach Resort
(Machafushi)

Kuda Rah

⑨

⑧

Dhigurah

Fenfushi

Mamigili

Ari Beach Resort
(Diddhu Finolhu)

Nalaguraidhoo
Holiday Island
(Dhiffushi)

Ariyaddhu Channel

Popular Dive Sites
① Manta Point
② Hammerhead Sharks
③ Mayaafushi Thila
④ Sting Ray City
⑤ Kandolodhu Reef
⑥ Fesdu Wreck
⑦ Fish Head Reef
⑧ Three thilas
⑨ Manta Point

■ Resorts
● Inhabited Island
○ Reef
○ Lagoon

The Atolls of Maldives

62.5 miles / 100 km

NORTH THILADHANMATHI ATOLL

SOUTH THILADHANMATHI ATOLL

MAKUNUDU

NORTH MILADHUMADULU ATOLL

ALIFUSHI

RAA ATOLL

SOUTH MILADHUMADULU ATOLL

LHAVIYANI ATOLL

BAA ATOLL

KASHIDU

GOIDU

GAARFARU

NORTH MALÉ ATOLL

THODDU

RASDU

Malé ✈

SOUTH MALÉ ATOLL

ARI ATOLL

FELIDHU ATOLL

NORTH NILANDHE ATOLL

MULAKU ATOLL

SOUTH NILANDHE ATOLL

KOLHUMADULU ATOLL

LAAMU ATOLL

HUVADHOO ATOLL

San'a YEMEN · Arabian · INDIA
· Bangalore
DJIBOUTI · Aden · Sea
· Addis
Ababa · SOMALIA · MALDIVES · Colombo ·
ETHIOPIA · Malé · SRI LANKA
KENYA · Mogadishu
· Nairobi
· Dodoma · Chagos Is. (U.K.)
· Dar es Salaam · SEYCHELLES
TANZANIA
COMOROS · Indian
MOZAM-
BIQUE · MADAGASCAR · Ocean
Antana-narivo · MAURITIUS
Reunion (Fr.)

Equa▶

FUA MULAKU ATOLL

Reef

ADDU ATOLL

Island

MALDIVES

Written and Presented by **Shoo-Yin Lim**

INSIGHT *pocket* GUIDES

Insight Pocket Guide:

Maldives

Directed by
Hans Höfer

Managing Editor
Francis Dorai

Edited by
Denise Tackett

Photography by
Didier Noirot and Larry Tackett

Design Concept by
V. Barl

Design by
Laddawan Wong

© 1994 APA Publications (HK) Ltd

All Rights Reserved

Printed in Singapore by
Höfer Press (Pte) Ltd
Fax: 65-8616438

Distributed in the UK & Ireland by
GeoCenter International UK Ltd
The Viables Center, Harrow Way
Basingstoke, Hampshire RG22 4BJ
ISBN: 9-62421-585-5

Worldwide distribution enquiries:
Höfer Communications Pte Ltd
38 Joo Koon Road
Singapore 2262
ISBN: 9-62421-585-5

Maruhaba!

Shoo-Yin Lim

My first brief encounter with Maldives was in 1985 when I booked myself out of urban madness to this land of lotus eaters for a much-needed holiday. Since then I've returned time and time again – to work and play – each visit more heart-wrenching when I have to leave.

More than 200,000 tourists come in search of paradise lost each year; few leave disappointed. The secluded islands, transparent waters and Maldives' reputation as a top diving spot are its strongest selling points. The 1,190 minuscule islands that make up Maldives are scattered over a wide area of endless sea. There are no great cities, monuments or historical sites to visit, and nightlife is virtually non-existent. If you plan to hop on a boat and play Robinson Crusoe on a deserted isle, think again; government restrictions make contact with local people difficult, and independent travel can be expensive. Given this scenario, the choice of an island resort is an important decision as you will spend most of your time on and around one. If you do not plan to dive and snorkel, or engage in watersports, or have a peculiar difficulty basking under the sun with a good book in hand, you had better give the islands a miss. In the *Resorts* section which kicks off this book, I've suggested 12 which cater to varying tastes and budgets in North and South Malé and Ari atolls, where most resorts are found. Also included is a tour to the capital island of Malé, and tips on shopping and eating out. As many come to dive, a major section of this book is devoted to this sport. Denise Tackett, who's done about 400 dives in these waters, tells you all about diving in the principal atolls. For suggestions on island-hopping, fishing, cruising and watersports, read the *Activities* section. Nature captivates with her magical charm on these islands, whether it's the unspoilt natural beauty of the islands or the teeming underwater world. If you have come in search of paradise, you'll find it here. I know I have. *Maruhaba – Welcome!*

Contents

*Preceding pages: Kuda Bandos, one of
1,190 islands that make up Maldives* **8**

Following pages:
a school of orange basslets

National emblem

HISTORY

Hanging like a garland below the southern tip of India is Maldives with its 1,190 tropical islands. Although little is known of its early history, Maldives is reputed to be one of the oldest states in the world. But for the many visitors who make it to these shores, the appeal of the islands lie not in the historical, but the natural. Quintessential tropical islands with soft white sands, swaying palms and transparent waters teeming with marine life are its biggest draws.

Early Origins

Strategically located at the crossroads of the major East-West trade routes, Maldives was a familiar port-of-call for many early seafaring civilizations. A reference to Maldives is first found in the work of Ptolemy, the Greek geographer, in AD2. It shows up again in the late 4th century works of Pappus of Alexandria and Scholasticus, a Theban who mentioned the many islands and their dangerous reefs that attracted unwary ships.

Maldives once dominated the cowrie trade

In the 9th and 10th century, Persian and Arab travellers mention the queens who ruled these islands, and the local abundance of cowries (small shells used as money). For centuries, Maldives was widely known as the centre of the cowrie trade. Today, two small cowries appear on the lower left hand corner of all Maldivian bank notes, a tribute to their former importance to this island state.

Maldives was known to the Chinese as the 'submerged Liu mountains' by the time of the Ming Dynasty (1368–1644). On an expedition to east Africa in 1433, explorer Ma Huan referred to Maldives as a big supplier of rope to seafarers, and he writes that the islands are the 'weak waters' referred to in the 5th century BC *Classic History*. Europeans knew very little of Maldives until 1498 when navigator Vasco da Gama became the first European to sail into the Indian Ocean.

Culture

11th-century Buddha head

There is much speculation about the origins of the first Maldivians, but it is generally agreed that early settlers came from Sri Lanka and southern India, followed later by Aryans from northern India. By 500BC Buddhism and Hinduism had arrived. Archaeological excavations, by British archaeologist H C P Bell in the 1920s and by Norwegian explorer Thor Heyerdahl in the 1980s, uncovered many relics to support these findings. Among the most revealing of Bell's findings were some Buddhist manuscripts and the head of a Buddha statue dating back to the 11th century.

Divehi script

Divehi, the national language, seems to verify these speculations. It is derived from the Indo-Iranian language group and is closely related to the ancient *Sinhala* language of Sri Lanka. *Divehi* also contains many words of Tamil and Arabic origin. The written form of *Thaana* has 24 characters, including nine Arabic numerals and some Tamil-originated words. The word 'Maldives' itself probably came from the Sanskrit word *Maladiv*, meaning 'garland of islands'. Like their language, which reflects the influence of the ancient seafarers, Maldivians today are a mixed race.

Heyerdahl theorizes that Maldives was inhabited as early as 2000BC by a mysterious race called the Redin. They worshipped the sun, built large temples and left behind images and scripts similar to those of an ancient Indus Valley civilization. Their temples were replaced with Buddhist temples which were themselves destroyed after the conversion to Islam in AD1153.

Conversion to Islam

Of all the early travellers, there is little doubt that the Arabs had the most influence and contributed to the most significant historical event in Maldives – the introduction of Islam in AD1153. The Islamic conversion is recounted in a well-known

An Arabic tombstone epitaph

Detail from Grand Mosque

story by the Arab traveller Ibn Battuta. At that time, the sea-demon Rannamari had been terrorizing the people of Malé. In order to appease the demon, the natives sacrificed a young virgin at the temple each month. A Moroccan traveller by the name of Abu'al Barakath who was staying in Malé learnt of the demon and took the place of the young girl at the temple one night. Throughout the night, Barakath recited the *Quran* and when the demon arrived, it was so frightened by the chanting of prayers that it disappeared into the sea, never to return again.

Whatever the veracity of this story, the Maldivian king Kalaminja was so impressed that he embraced Islam and declared it the common religion in the country. To this day, Barakath is much venerated and his tomb stands in Malé as a holy shrine.

From Sultanate to Republic

After the adoption of Islam in 1153, three sultanic dynasties – which included three female rulers – peacefully ruled the country for the next 400 years. In 1517, Sultan Kalu Muhammad signed a treaty with the Portuguese, allowing them to establish an unpopular trading post in Malé. With the help of some Indian corsairs, the Maldivians succeeded in destroying the post, only to have the Portuguese retaliate by sending a small armada to build a fort in Malé.

The next sultan, Hassan IX, was influenced by the Portuguese and converted to Christianity while on a trip to India. His efforts to convert key Maldivians to Christianity in 1552 failed when his sympathizers were seized. This incurred the wrath of the Portuguese, and in 1558, Captain Andreas Andre invaded Maldives. The occupation lasted for 15 years and was marked by brutality, despair and an on-going guerrilla war. The Portuguese were finally ousted in 1573 when three brothers from Utheemu island led a rebellion and killed the whole garrison – shortly before the deadline for Maldivians to convert to Christianity or face certain death. Muhammed Thakurufaanu, one of the brothers who led the rebellion, became the next sultan and introduced many reforms, including the minting of coins and the establishment of a militia. Maldives has not been ruled by a foreign power since and today, Thakurufaanu is regarded as the greatest national hero.

In 1645, diplomatic ties were established with the Dutch who who had ousted the Portuguese as the dominant power in the Indian Ocean. In exchange for cowries, Maldives received supplies of spices, areca nuts and ammunition from the Dutch. In

An 1886 newspaper article

1752–3, a small expedition headed by Ali Raja from south India tried to invade Maldives but was repelled with the help of a small French fleet. By 1796, the British had taken control of Sri Lanka from the Dutch, and trade between Malé and Colombo flourished. Borah merchants from India came to dominate almost all trade in Maldives by mid-19th century. Resentment and jealousy among the locals soon led to trouble and riots. In 1887, the local businessmen revolted and burned down the shops and warehouses of these merchants. At the same time, Sultan Muhammed Mu'inuddin signed a treaty which made Maldives a British Protectorate.

In 1932, Sultan Muhammed Shamsuddeen III was obliged, in exchange for British recognition, to accept a written constitution which limited his power and introduced the concept of elections. Hassan Nooraddeen II became the first elected sultan.

Sultan Muhammed Shamsuddeen III (second from left)

Ten years later, the constitution was rewritten but the elected sultan declined to serve. Prime Minister Muhammed Amin Didi took over and led a modernization program which led to the establishment of the National Security Service and the nationalization of fish exports. The Sultanate was abolished in 1953 and Amin Didi became the first President. Food shortages, a ban on tobacco and riots led to his downfall and the demise of the constitution. In 1954, Muhammed Farid Didi took the throne and became the last sultan.

In 1948, Maldives signed a defence agreement with the British, giving them control of foreign affairs while maintaining control of domestic affairs. During World War II the British built airstrips in Gan and Kelai to protect their interests. Many Maldivians were employed at the Gan airstrip and in 1956 the British were granted a 100-year lease on it. The following year, the newly-elected President Ibrahim Nasir revoked the lease, unleashing a revolt of the southernmost atolls against the government. In 1959, the three southern atolls seceded from Maldives and formed the United Suvadive Islands, prompting Nasir to re-negotiate the air base lease with the British. In 1962, Nasir invaded the United Suvadive Islands and forced their president to flee to Seychelles.

On 26 July 1965, the British relinquished their role as protector. Maldives became an independent nation and joined the United Nations. Three years later, a new constitution was drawn up and Maldives became a republic with Nasir as its first president. By 1972, the constitution was amended to increase the president's powers. The same year, foreign currency controls instituted by Sri Lanka caused the collapse of the dried fish market – Maldives' biggest export. Fortunately for Maldives, tourism arrived with the

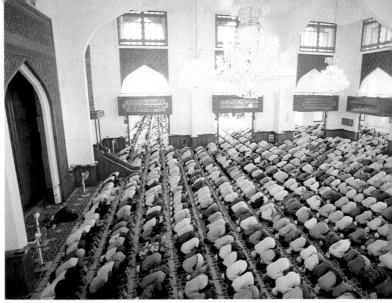

Friday prayer scene at the Grand Mosque

opening of two resorts on Kurumba and Bandos. The benefits generated by the new industry, however, did not filter down to the common people. Accused of using government funds for his own use, Nasir fled the country in 1978, taking with him a large part of the Maldives treasury.

In 1978, Maumoon Abdul Gayoom was elected President. He has been re-elected three times since then, most recently in 1993. Despite three attempted coups, Gayoom has significantly improved the standard of living throughout the country, especially in the areas of health, education and communication. His open door policy and international programmes have brought significant changes and international recognition to Maldives.

Governing by Faith

Maldives is a Muslim country and its inhabitants are Sunni Muslims of the Shafi'ite sect, one of the most liberal of all Islamic sects. Life and religion are completely integrated and the Islamic law is the law of the land.

The five pillars of Islam are adhered to throughout the islands. They are: the affirmation that 'there is no God but God and Mohammed is His prophet'; prayer five times a day; alms-giving; dawn-to-sundown fasting during the month of *Ramadan*; and if possible, to make the pilgrimage to Mecca.

From a very young age, the Maldivian learns the fundamental principles of Islam and recites the *Quran*. On Fridays, the men don their best for the *hukuru namaad* or Friday prayers to reaffirm their faith in Allah while the women pray in separate mosques or at home. The consumption of pork and alcohol are prohib-

A moment of reflection

ited. Fasting during *Ramadan* is strictly observed and working hours are rescheduled to accommodate this difficult period.

The practice of Islam is relatively liberal here. Maldives is governed by Islamic law or *shari'a*, but maximum punishments are not handed out. The usual sentence is banishment to another atoll for a period of time – the thought being that there is no worse punishment than to be separated from one's family. For crimes of adultery and alcohol consumption, a form of flogging is added to the banishment, but it does not hurt – it is done more to make an example of the person rather than to hurt him.

Divorces are easy to obtain and Maldives is known to have the highest divorce rate in the world, a reason which perhaps explains why marriages here are generally not elaborate celebrations. No stigma is attached to divorce, perhaps because it is a carry-over from the days of old when seafarers would stop here, take a temporary wife and divorce her before setting sail again.

Despite their strong faith, many Maldivians are traditionally superstitious and believe in *dhevi*, supernatural spirits found in nature. Recitations from the *Quran*, potions and spells from a *hakeem* or medicine man are used to drive them away.

Maldivian Dance

Bodu beru, or big drum, is the most popular form of traditional entertainment in Maldives. The drum is made from a hollowed-out coconut tree, covered in goatskin and held together by a coir rope. *Bodu beru* is performed by two or three drummers and a singer, and all the men join in to dance. There is a fine tradition

Frenetic beating of the bodu beru

of male dancing here and *bodu beru* encourages creative expression.

The spirited music starts off with a slow beat and gradually works up to a frenetic pace. The loud, rhythmic beat encourages more dancers to join in as the pace picks up. *Bodu beru* originated years ago when seafarers from Africa, Arabia and Indonesia stopped here on their voyages and shared their local song and dance customs with the Maldivians. Over time, the meaning of the words to the songs have been lost, but the spirit remains. *Bodu beru* performances may be seen at some resorts which organise weekly cultural performances for tourists.

Other less common dances include *tharaa*, or tambourine, a dance introduced by the Gulf Arabs and *dhanndhi jehun*, both performed by men only. The *bandiyaa jehun* is an adaptation of the Indian pot dance. Performed only by young women, the dancers beat their fingers against the metal water pots they carry. It is a popular dance on Thoddu, an island to the west of North Malé Atoll.

Living with Nature

While the sea provides Maldivians with food, shelter and jobs – fishing accounts for more than 70 percent of total exports – it also wreaks havoc on these small, exposed islands. Fierce storms and tidal swells are known throughout the country. In 1987, a huge tidal swell flooded parts of Malé and washed away much of the newly-reclaimed land. Many islands, including the airport, were flooded and damage was substantial. A breakwater, consisting of

20,000 three-ton cement tetrapods, was constructed along the south side of Malé in an effort to protect the island from future tidal swells.

But even that may not be enough to save Maldives if scientists are correct in their predictions of global warming and rising sea levels. Most of the islands are less than 2m (6½ft) above sea level and even a small rise in the ocean will inundate many of them. It has been speculated that at the present rate of sea-level rise, Maldives could be completely wiped out one day.

The global warming issue is further exacerbated by that of coral mining. For years, coral has been mined from the shallow reefs for use as building ma-

Illegal coral miners

terial. Pressure from the increasing population and a new affluence among Maldivians has led to an increased demand for mined coral for new houses and buildings. Realizing the folly in mining the fringing reefs which protect the islands from the pounding surf, the government has set aside certain reefs for mining and is assessing penalties for those caught mining outside the designated areas.

President Gayoom has been especially vocal in bringing the plight of low-lying island countries to the attention of the developed world. With the assistance of the United Nations, Maldives has developed a National Action Plan designed to manage and maintain the environment with a view to the future.

1992 was dedicated to the environment

Historical Highlights

1153 King Kalaminja declares Islam the national religion.

1343 The Theemuge dynasty is replaced by the Veeru Umaru dynasty.

1517 The Portuguese establish a trading post in Malé.

1558 The Portuguese, led by Capt Andreas Andre, invade Maldives. Andre tries to convert Maldivians to Christianity.

1573 The Portuguese are ousted in a rebellion. Militia established and first coins minted.

1602 Frenchman Francois Pyrard de Laval is shipwrecked and taken prisoner for five years. He later publishes a three-volume account of his observations in Maldives.

1645 Maldives establishes diplomatic contacts with the Dutch Governor of Sri Lanka.

1759 Following the death of Sultan Imaadhudheen III, Izzudeen becomes the first Sultan of the Huraage dynasty.

1796 The British take over from the Dutch in Sri Lanka. Trade between Male and Colombo increases.

1879 H C P Bell shipwrecked in Maldives.

1887 Local uprising against Borah merchants. Maldives is declared a British Protectorate.

1906 First post-office opens.

1920 H C P Bell returns to carry out archaeological excavations.

1932 The first written constitution is drawn up.

1942 British establish two airstrips during World War II.

1943 Sultan Abdul Majeed Didi abdicates. Amin Didi assumes power. The National Security Service is set up and fish exports are nationalised.

1948 A mutual defence pact is signed with the British.

1954 Sultanate reinstated. Last sultan takes the throne.

1953 The Sultanate is abolished. Amin Didi becomes the first President of Maldives.

1956 The British negotiate a 100-year lease on their air base on Gan.

1957 Ibrahim Nasir is elected Prime Minister. His call for a review of the British Occupation is met with protest. Three southern atolls break away to form a separate state called United Suvadive Islands.

1960 Maldives grants the British a 30-year lease of Gan.

1962 Nasir sents a fleet to attack the United Suvadive Islands.

1965 On 26 July, British relinquish their role. Maldives becomes fully independent and joins the UN.

1968 Sultanate is abolished and republican constitution is adopted. Nasir becomes President of second Republic.

1972 Market for dried fish collapses. First two resorts open.

1978 Nasir flees to Singapore with a huge part of the government's coffer. Maumoon Abdul Gayoom is elected President.

1980 Coup against Gayoom aborted.

1981–82 Malé airport opens.

1982 Thor Heyerdahl begins excavations in southern atolls.

1983 The Maldives is made a special member of the Commonwealth of Nations. Gayoom is re-elected. A second coup attempt aborted.

1985 Meeting of Commonwealth Finance Ministers.

1987 Tidal swell causes flooding and beach erosion throughout.

1988 Gayoom is re-elected for a second term. A third coup is foiled.

1989 'Small States Conference' is held in Malé, in view of the dangers posed by global warming.

1990 Maldives celebrates 25 years of independence. Breakwater on south side of Malé is completed.

1992 Adopted as the SAARC (South Asian Association of Regional Co-operation) Year of the Environment. Maldives participates in the Earth Summit at Rio de Janerio.

1993 Gayoom is re-elected for a fourth term.

RESORTS

About 90 percent of visitors – the majority of whom come here to dive – spend their time at resorts on one- to two-week packages with everything arranged, including airfare. Most are Europeans, with Germans and Italians forming over 40 percent of the tourist population. Maldives is also gaining popularity with Asians, mainly young Japanese vacationers, and Australians.

Although there are more than 1,190 tiny islands in Maldives, accommodation for tourists is limited to some 70 developed resorts and the capital island of Malé, carefully distanced from the 200 or so islands inhabited by Maldivians. The independent tourist is a rare sight in Maldives. Apart from the resorts and Malé, all other islands are out of bounds: to visit one involves a difficult process of applying for a special permit from the Department of Atoll Administration in Malé.

Only designated inhabited islands around the resorts are open for visits during the day: staying overnight is strictly prohibited. The government-imposed restrictions are part of a conscious effort to prevent visitors from disrupting the local Muslim life.

Each island houses only one resort, except Kuramathi in Ari Atoll which has three resorts on the same island. As a general rule, the name of the island is also the name of the resort, although there are exceptions like Club Med which sits on the island of Farukolhufushi and Kurumba resort on Vihamana Fushi. In such cases, the islands are usually referred to by their resort names.

Selecting a resort is an important consideration as you will spend most of your time on and around your chosen island resort. Activities such as visits to

Make diving your top priority

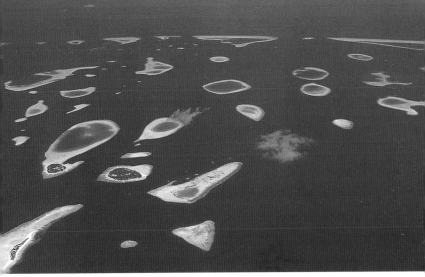

Most resorts are concentrated on North and South Malé and Ari atolls

inhabited islands and Malé, picnic and snorkelling excursions, and a full range of watersports are offered by all resorts. Practically every resort has its own dive centre that conducts a range of courses by qualified instructors. Find out from your travel agent what sports facilities are available and their rental charges. Some offer free windsurfing and sailing lessons and unlimited use of these facilities while others may charge an hourly or weekly rental fee.

The 70 resorts in Maldives are located mainly within the central North and South Malé and Ari atolls, two-thirds of which are concentrated in the first two atolls. A handful of other resorts are scattered over Felidhu, Lhaviyani and Addu atolls. Ari Atoll was designated the New Tourism Zone by the government in 1988. Since then, there has been a rash of new resorts here, many of which cater to Italians. Because of the 64-km (40-mile) distance from Malé, transfers to Ari Atoll resorts are either by speedboat, or helicopter to the nearest helipad and then a short *dhoni* ride to your resort.

Room rates vary greatly among resorts, and from season to season. During the high season from November to April, the double room price range of US$70 to US$450 will buy you anything from a basic shower and bed to the sinfully luxurious.

Ari Beach helipad

In terms of atmosphere, it can range from the holiday-camp rowdiness of Club Med to the tranquil upmarket surroundings of Nika, which boasts a private stretch of beach for each of its 25 bungalows. In general, accommodation is in bungalows with thatched or tiled roofs, or terraced blocks with a fine stretch of beach in front. While fresh water was considered an indulgence some years back, most resorts today have desalination plants, and some even have the luxury of hot baths. The last few years have seen a tremendous

Comfortable accommodation at Kanifinolhu

effort at upgrading and renovating at many resorts. Air-conditioning, mini-bars, telephones, and even piped-in music have become standard fixtures at some of the better ones. In some of the more sophisticated (read expensive) resorts you will find fresh-water swimming pools, jacuzzis, saunas, tennis courts and gymnasiums.

Most tour packages include transfers between airport and resort, accommodation, meals and some sports activities. Bed and breakfast, half-board and full-board packages are available. For the majority of visitors, the food options are confined to the resort they are staying at. Many resorts have only one main restaurant and only full-board packages. Menu choices can be limited but there are usually a number of western-style buffets served during the week. Some of the larger resorts may have an additional coffee-house, restaurant or grill for added variety.

Bars are usually well-stocked with spirits and beer, although locals are banned from consuming liquor. In addition, most resorts have a boutique that sells a range of souvenir items, beachwear, and daily essentials should you run out of them.

Night entertainment is limited, and in many cases, non-existent. On some

Buffet at Rihiveli

resorts, a live band or a Maldivian cultural show is featured once or twice a week. On other days, a disco night is organized.

Resorts are generally booked from the visitor's home country and the choice is limited by what the travel agencies can offer. Bear in mind that some resorts may be leased out to specific tour agencies catering to a particular nationality. For example, several resorts have a German-only or Italian-only clientele. Some of the major flagships operators in Europe include Meier's Weltreisen, TUI, Franco Rosso, Hotelplan, Turisanda, Kuoni, Club Vacanze and Club Méditerranée. You may also book direct with the representative office in Malé if you decide to plan your own holiday.

You will find a wide variation between prices quoted by resorts and travel agents. Large tour operators will offer hefty discounts off published rates. Shop around for the best deal and be on the lookout for specials during the low season, when prices can drop by as much as 50 percent. Inquire with your agent whether meals are part of the package.

Bearing in mind differing tastes, I have made a selection of re-

Arriving at a resort

sorts that will appeal to most people. Other resorts of note are listed in the *Practical Information* section under '*Accommodation*'. Invariably, one's enjoyment is determined by the people around, and during the peak season, this can mean 50 to 200 or more people squeezed into one small island.

Keep in mind the house rules, no nude-bathing (this is a Muslim country), no collection of corals from the reefs, and no fishing on the house reefs. Rest assured that no matter where you choose to stay in Maldives, you can be certain of a few good things – lots of sunshine, fine sandy beaches washed by a clear lagoon and stunning coral reefs.

Note: When the island name differs from that of the resort, it is indicated within parenthesis. Price ranges indicated here are for a standard double room (with full board, unless otherwise stated) for one night during the high season:
$=under US$150; *$$*=US$151–US$200; *$$$*=US$201–US$250; *$$$$*=above US$250

Perfecting the art of relaxation

North Malé Atoll

1. Kurumba (Vihamana Fushi)

No of rooms: 170; Distance from airport: 3km (1¾ miles); Price range: $$ (breakfast only); Local Agent: Universal Enterprises Ltd, 38 Orchid Magu, Malé. Tel: 32-2971, Fax: 32-2678

Aerial view of Kurumba

Maldives' first resort opened on the island of Vihamana Fushi in 1972. **Kurumba** (meaning 'young coconut') is the closest resort to Malé, and is ideal for travellers wishing to mix business with pleasure. There is a convention centre for 500 guests and a fully-equipped business centre. The resort has a large fleet of speedboats for hire, providing quick and efficient transfers to and from Malé in less than 10 minutes.

The 1½-km (1-mile) long island is beautifully landscaped with hibiscus and bougainvillaea shrubs, and frangipani and coconut trees, lending it a distinct tropical atmosphere. Since 1985, the resort has undergone massive upgrading. The 170 rooms and suites are tastefully furnished, with all the necessary mod-cons like air-conditioning, hot and cold baths, hair-dryers, IDD telephones and mini-bars.

While food and its lack of variety is a common complaint at many resorts, Kurumba prides itself on having five restaurants that offer several cuisines. Guests from Malé and other resorts sometimes hop over to this resort for a Chinese dinner at the Ming Court or a North Indian meal at the Kurumba Ma-

A growing number of resorts now have swimming pools

hal. Besides the main restaurant and an up-market continental restaurant, there is a 24-hour coffee-house for those who get peckish in the middle of the night. My personal favourite is the open-air terrace where you can enjoy fresh Maldivian lobsters while your toes dig into the sand under the star-lit sky. A nightly discotheque offers after-dinner entertainment.

Kurumba has a comprehensive list of sports facilities such as windsurfing, waterskiing, snorkelling, night fishing and glass bottom boats to explore the reefs around the island. The scuba-diving school is run by Eurodivers, one of the biggest dive operators in the islands. In addition, there is a fitness centre equipped with a jacuzzi, two flood-lit tennis courts and billiard rooms. A fresh-water swimming pool completes the picture; an unnecessary intrusion given the crystal clear lagoon surrounding the island.

Although ranking high in terms of comfort and efficiency, it is exactly the many modern trappings that sometimes rob a resort of its restive away-from-it-all feeling. Sadly, this seems to be a trend with some new resorts in Maldives. Bow-tied waiters on a tropical island in the middle of the Indian Ocean are a bit over the top!

Ming Court restaurant

2. Bandos

No of rooms: 203; Distance from airport: 8km (5 miles);
Price range: $$$; Local Agent: Bandos Malé Office, H Jazeera,
Marine Drive, Malé. Tel: 32-2844, Fax: 32-1026

Like Kurumba, Bandos first opened in 1972 and has undergone many changes since. Just 15 minutes from the airport by speedboat, Bandos is one of the biggest resorts with 203 rooms. This is a relatively large island though one side of it is quite rocky and has no beach. Nearby is the uninhabited island of Kuda Bandos, which is reserved for the locals as a public park on Fridays. During the rest of the week, Kuda Bandos is frequented by tourists from nearby resorts and is an ideal spot for excursions and picnics.

The overall design of the resort is very modern. The reception complex, the main restaurant, coffee-house, shops, bar and swimming pool are the focal points on the island. The air-conditioned

rooms are situated away from the activity centres in blocks of two or more and arranged in a rather odd manner. Though each room is touted as beach-front, the beach can be about 50m (55yds) away from your doorstep. The interiors are spacious, with wide glass panels that allow a generous view of the surroundings.

The coffee-house serves a good selection of Western and Asian fare. For dinner, there is the Pasta Place and the Harbour Grill. Don't forget to try the Bandos' homemade ice-cream if you are there, definitely one of the best treats in Maldives.

The resort is home to the only Aquascope in Maldives. This is a submarine-like underwater explorer that offers non-divers and

children an opportunity to see the fascinating colourful reefs around the island. The excellent house reef is ideal for snorkelling. There is also the full range of watersports like scuba diving, windsurfing, waterskiing and sailing. Bandos is one of the few resorts in Maldives that offer parasailing.

Bandos has its own shopping gallery with souvenir shops, a photo-shop for quick processing, a gem shop and a beauty

Ride the Aquascope

salon. The sports complex is well-equipped with a gymnasium, tennis courts and the only squash courts in Maldives. Bandos also has a clinic with a full-time doctor for basic medical consultation. The Swiss-AMDC Clinic in Malé, together with Bandos, recently installed a 2-man recompression chamber on the island.

Over the last few years, Bandos has gained a reputation as a stop-over hotel for airline crews. In actual fact, it attracts a mixed clientele from Europe and Asia, from boisterous families to wide-eyed honeymooners. Good service and a friendly staff contribute to the holiday feel of the island, as do little surprises like the crowing of a rooster to start off the day.

3. Kanifinolhu

No of rooms: 125; Distance from airport: 16km (10 miles);
Price range: $; Local agent: Cyprea Pte Ltd, 25, Marine Drive,
Malé. Tel: 32-2451, Fax: 32-3523

Located on the eastern reef of North Malé Atoll, Kanifinolhu is 15½km (9½ miles) long and 180m (180yds) wide, with an extensive lagoon ideal for sailing and windsurfing and a wide stretch of beach to laze on. Designed with the aim of achieving a fine balance

Popular with young Germans and close to good diving spots

between the traditional and the modern, there is a strong emphasis on the preservation of the natural surroundings. As there are no breakwaters to obstruct your view you can look out to the horizon and feel the expanse of the ocean. The use of wood is prominent throughout the resort's main building, especially in the reception area with its wide posts and beams. If you cannot live without air-conditioning, you should know that only the more expensive deluxe rooms are artificially cooled.

The island is covered with thick vegetation, and over time, the newly-planted coconut trees along the beach will grow to provide a curtain of green from the sea. In the open area outside the bar, there is a century-old banyan tree referred to as *l'arme d'ile* (weapon of the island). Under its thick shade, guests often seek relief from the hot Maldivian sun to enjoy a cool drink and while away the afternoon.

Relaxing outside the bar

Most guests, mainly young Germans, come to Kanifinolhu on a full-board basis. The food in the main restaurant is nothing to rave about though. For a change, try the coffee-house on the other end of the island. The chef bakes the best local bread I've tasted and tosses a mean Sultan salad, a simple mixture of grated coconut, tuna and a local grass. The wooden platform facing the open sea makes an ideal setting for a romantic candlelight dinner.

Kanifinolhu is the base for the well-established Eurodivers and is near to some of the best diving spots in the area. Apart from para-sailing and the usual watersports, the resort recently acquired a new fishing boat. The owners, Cyprea Travels, also operate a boat called *Discovery*. This is used mainly for diving safaris, but special cruises can be arranged on request.

Bird's eye view of Vabbinfaru

4. Vabbinfaru Paradise Island

No of rooms: 30; Distance from airport: 16km (10 miles);
Price range: $$$$; Local agent: Dhirham, Faamudheyri, Malé.
Tel: 32-3369, Fax: 32-4752

Managed by a French family aptly named Paris, Vabbinfaru is one
of the prettiest islands in North Malé Atoll, with fine talcum pow-
der sand that seems to melt beneath your feet. Situated about an
hour away by *dhoni* from the airport, Vabbinfaru sets its time one
hour ahead of Malé time, allowing guests to take advantage of an
extra hour of daylight.

Like its neighbours Baros and Ihuru, Vabbinfaru has one of the
best house reefs around, thriving with an abundance of corals and
a myriad of colourful fishes which swim in the shallow lagoon.

Smaller resorts like Vabbinfaru are more appealing because they
tend to be more restful. The 30 bungalows are set back from sandy
avenues luxuriantly overgrown with thick screwpines and coconut
palms. The bungalows are circular in shape
and very Maldivian in style with their white-
washed coral walls and thatched roofs made
from *cadjan* – overlapping palms woven together and firmly bound by coir rope. The
rooms are simply furnished with ceiling
fans, and the showers have fresh water.

The resort employs a few Europeans to
cater to its largely Italian (and some
French and Japanese) clientele, but it is
really the Maldivian staff in their batik shirts and
lunghis that give the resort a very local feel. The emphasis is on
food; with the lunch buffet comprising a selection of pastas, salads,

Maldivian staff

grilled fish and curries served under the cool shade of the trees. Dinner, announced by the blowing of a conch, calls for a little more decorum in the restaurant and guests are reminded to dress appropriately for the occasion.

In general, there is a lazy atmosphere at the resort, in rhythm with the Maldivian pace of life. The island is definitely not for those keen on orga-

Vabbinfaru has a well-stocked boutique

nized activities and mass participation. Though a range of activities are available, there is no gung-ho instructor pressing you to sign up for courses or excursions. The only drawback is that with a lack of eager participants, it is sometimes difficult to find the minimum number of people required for an island-hopping excursion or a boat dive. Most of the time, guests can be found amusing themselves with a game of backgammon or darts near the bar, or else, finessing their tans by the beach.

Plans are presently underway for a major refurbishment, expected to take place at time of press. Vabbinfaru has great potential with its superbly beautiful surroundings, fine beach and lagoon. If ever there was a honeymoon destination, this is it.

5. Club Med (Farukolufushi)

No of rooms: 152; Distance from airport: 2km (1¼ miles);
Price range: $ per person, most sports facilities included;
Local agent: No 1, Ibrahim Hassan Didi Magu, Majeedee Baazaar,
Malé. Tel: 32-2976, Fax: 32-2850

One of the most crowded resorts in Maldives, Club Med Farukolufushi is striking for its architectural features. The curved roof of the main building is shaped like the hull of a traditional Maldivian *dhoni*. Rising tall over the trees, it is the first structure you see from a distance. Close-up though, one notices its rather frayed edges.

Like other Club Med resorts found all over the world, this one attracts a largely French and Japanese clientele and is run by a team of GOs (Gentile Organizers)

Club Med's distinctive roof

who look after the needs of its guests. Club Med caters to those with an insatiable need for noise and fun, though why hordes of Japanese honeymooners would want to come here defies the imagination.

The air-conditioned rooms are spartanly-furnished and grouped into 19 double-storey terraced blocks. Showers have fresh water. There is a whole range of organized activities to keep you on your feet – mini-Olympics, regattas, volleyball matches and singing competitions. While nightlife is rare in most resorts, the Club has its own in-house entertainment, usually a show staged by a GO team and a nightly disco.

Overall, Club Med offers good value for money. The all-inclusive package allows guests to try their hands (and feet) at a whole range of sports activities such as windsurfing and sailing at no extra cost. The large, shallow lagoon is ideal for sailing and windsurfing. The emphasis at this resort though is on diving. Eurodivers runs the diving school, one of the biggest in Maldives. In the high season, as many as three diving boats go out in a day.

The resort also ranks high in terms of food, with an international team of chefs turning out a very palatable spread for every meal. There is a special Japanese corner which serves *sushi* and *sashimi*. The free flow of French wine and beer will help wash all that food down, if the endless string of organized activities do not.

Popular with Japanese honeymooners

Right: set sail in the sunset

South Malé Atoll

6. Rihiveli

No of rooms: 40; Distance from airport: 40km (25 miles);
Price range: $$$$; Local agent: Imad's Agencies, Jawahiriyya,
Chandhani Magu, Malé. Tel: 32-3441, Fax: 32-6924

Behind every memorable resort is a group of unforget-
table personalities that set it apart. Rihiveli
is one such resort. There is big Babar, an
imposing yet gentle giant and his parrots
behind the bar. There is Paulo, the dreamer
who found paradise here and now lives on
the island. And of course, there is Pitt

Babar and his parrot

Pietersoone who has been described as running the resort in an
autocratic manner. Since 1978, Pietersoone and his family have

Rihiveli rustic

lived on and managed Rihiveli in a highly
personalized style. The idea is to create a
'home away from home', he says, for the
small clientele (Italian, French and Swiss)
that has found its way here. At Rihiveli,
you will not find large organized groups;
in fact Pietersoone discourages them.

Some 45 minutes by speedboat from
the airport, Rihiveli, (meaning 'silver
sands') is the southernmost resort in
South Malé Atoll. The resort is fringed

by three tiny uninhabited islands. The waters around Rihiveli are so
shallow that it is possible to wade across to these islands for picnics
and barbecues on the beach, a refreshing change from eating in the
main restaurant. Not that the latter is any less an option, with its
open view of the sea. On some mornings, you can enjoy breakfast
and watch the thrilling spectacle of flying fish out on their early

A delectable spread of French and Italian dishes

morning hunt. The food at Rihiveli is excellent, with a spread of mainly French and Italian dishes. Once a week, guests are encouraged to try the Maldivian buffet. A huge signboard outside the restaurant invites you to eat with your hands as the locals do.

Guests are housed in individual bungalows, with names such as *Anemone* or *Donemus* rather than plain numbers. The 40 cottages have a rustic feel with their white coral walls and high thatched roofs. Though not air-conditioned, the gentle sea breezes provide ample ventilation. A hammock outside each bungalow, perfect for that afternoon siesta, completes the picture of tropical paradise.

Although there is no house reef around the island, a *dhoni* brings guests out to a nearby reef for snorkelling. The diving centre run by Eurodivers is highly rated among resorts in Maldives for their personalized coaching. Windsurfing and sailing facilities are available free of charge, and yoga and aerobics classes are held in the evenings. Parasailing, fishing and waterskiing are available for a fee. Rihiveli also runs *Shadas*, the boat used by the Norwegian explorer Thor Heyerdahl on his expedition around the atolls. Cruises and diving safaris are organized if there is a minimum number of people.

7. Laguna Beach Resort (Velassaru)

No of rooms: 104; Distance from airport: 4km (2½ miles); Price range: $$ (breakfast only); Local agent: Universal Enterprises Ltd, 38 Orchid Magu, Malé. Tel: 32-2971, Fax: 32-2678

Going south from Malé, sailing past the islands of Villingili and Vaadhu, one arrives at Laguna Beach Resort, a 5-star resort opened in 1990. This is my favourite among the locally-owned Universal chain of resorts in terms of ambience and layout.

The reception area has a high ceiling and carries heavy Filipino accents in its design. Accommodation is in bungalow units, each separated by thick shrub and trees for privacy, or in double-storey blocks away from the main activity area. The deluxe rooms are attractively furnished, with a split-level lounge area and bedroom.

Housekeeping gets top marks at this resort. A leaking faucet was fixed within minutes after it was reported.

Laguna, which attracts a well-heeled cosmopolitan crowd, is blessed with a stretch of soft sandy beach all round the island. There is also a splendid lagoon

Laguna has a large lagoon

with thick clusters of soft brown corals and schools of colourful damselfish. The large lagoon is also ideal for windsurfing and sailing. There is a comprehensive list of sea and land activities to keep you on your feet, including two swimming pools and a hydro-pool to soothe tired muscles.

Like the other Universal-owned resorts, Laguna has a good number of restaurants – the main Summer Fields restaurant for guests booked on a half-board or full-board arrangement, a coffee-shop, an Italian restaurant, a Chinese restaurant with a Shanghainese chef, and a barbecue terrace overlooking the sea. An interesting theme buffet is held each week to add variety to the regular menu. Regular entertainment is provided in the bar with either a live band, disco or a weekly cultural dance performance.

8. Embudu Finolhu

No of rooms: 40; Distance from airport: 8km (5 miles);
Price range: $; Local agent: G Makhumaage, Malé.
Tel: 32-6483, Fax: 32-2634

Fifteen minutes by speedboat from the airport lies Embudu Finolhu, on the eastern rim of South Malé Atoll. This is a very narrow island with a large lagoon, managed by the Indian Taj Hotel group. Among the resorts I've visited so far, Embudu Finolhu takes the prize for being the coolest and most laid-back. There is no way you can even begin to think about work here! A few days on this resort is the best way to unwind, which is what the mixed European and Asian clientele seem to want.

This is a small resort with only 40 rooms, 24 of which are wooden water bungalows. Extending over the edge and building over the water has served the island well because it allows much of the greenery to be preserved. The overhanging branches of the trees form a charming archway along the main pathway of the island. The water bungalows are spacious and the feeling is enhanced by the unobstructed views of the sea from the wide balconies. A flight of stairs leads right down to the clear waters below. A little jetty at the other end of the island, away from the main area, is the perfect place to enjoy some solitude.

Even at the peak of the season, it is hard to imagine that there are more than 100 people on the island, except at mealtimes in the restaurant. The menu consists of mainly western dishes, though spe-

Embudu Finolhu water bungalows

cial requests for curried fish and rice can be made ahead. For diving enthusiasts, the Embudu Express site nearby promises one of the best drift dives in the area.

9. Fun Island Resort (Bodu Finolhu)

No of rooms: 100; Distance from airport: 38km (23½ miles);
Price range: $; Local agent: Villa Building, Ibrahim Hassan Didi
Magu, Malé. Tel: 32-4478, Fax: 32-7845

Bodu Finolhu, like many islands on the edge of the atoll, is a long and narrow island. On approaching the resort, one is struck by the long wooden jetty and the two islets across the channel where you may find a few guests serving their term of solitary sunbathing.

Extensively renovated in 1992, Fun Island Resort caters to varied nationalities – Europeans, Australians, Japanese and Taiwanese. The resort seems pretty popular with family groups, judging from the number of families there during my stay. In fact, the atmosphere reminded me of a summer holiday camp in Europe, with laundry lines hanging out side the terraced blocks and little children chasing each other down the beach. This is not your ideal get-away for peace and tranquillity. The island is tiny, measuring 30m by 800m (33yds by 870yds), but if it gets crowded here, you can easily walk over to the two, nearby uninhabited islands at low tide.

Bodu sits on the edge of the atoll

amily fun at Bodu

The rooms are set in terraced blocks of two to four rooms. Though not luxurious, you will find all that you need – air-conditioning, telephones, mini-bars, and hot and cold showers. The furnishings are a little garish though, with bright lime-green curtains and red plastic flowers on the wall. Aside from the main restaurant, there is a 24-hour coffee-house. The most pleasant part of the resort is the bar which opens out to a wooden patio overlooking the sea where you can enjoy the sunset with a cocktail in hand.

The resort offers the standard range of watersports facilities for a fee. Courses are conducted for windsurfing and catamaran sailing. The Delphis diving centre, run by a tall Dutch lady by the name of Rit, is well-established in Maldives. For the many Japanese guests, there is a Japanese dive instructor at hand.

ARI ATOLL

10. Kuramathi Cottage Club

*No of rooms: 30;
Distance from airport:
58km (36 miles);
Price range: $ (break-
fast only); Local
Agent: Universal
Enterprises Ltd, 38
Orchid Magu, Malé.
Tel: 32-2971,
Fax: 32-2678*

A 20-minute helicopter
transfer from Malé In-
ternational Airport
takes you to the fish-
ing village of Rasdhu,
just north of Ari Atoll.
From here, a waiting

Waterskiing past Kuramathi's jetty

dhoni picks up guests for a short ride to Kuramathi, a relatively big
island 15 minutes away. This is the only island where you can find
three different resorts – Kuramathi Cottage Club, Blue Lagoon and
Kuramathi Village – all run by the same management.

About 1½km (1 mile) long and 600m (655yds) wide, it takes
about an hour to walk around the whole island. Kuramathi island
is remarkably green; the vegetation rich with fruits trees, breadfruit, screwpine and banyan. Landscaping has added an abundance
of floral shrubs and colour to the natural beauty of the island.

The smallest of the three resorts, the Cottage Club is a neat-look-
ing village with 30 well-spaced out bungalows, each with a little
garden of its own. The resort manager, Hakurey, is an avid gar-
dener and is responsible for much of the beautiful greenery. His
green fingers have also nurtured a variety of fruit trees and fresh
vegetables at the resort nursery for meals.

Popular with Germans, the resort attracts a large number of repeat visitors. During my last visit, I met a German couple who had returned for the fifth time and, on an average, stay for about six weeks each time – a fact which speaks volumes for this resort and its charming atmosphere.

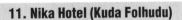

Nightlife at Kuramathi

Many sports facilities are shared among the three resorts. The snorkelling boat, for example, makes its round each morning to pick up guests from all three jetties. If you are an archery buff, you should know that this resort has the only archery range in Maldives. Divers will be captivated with the school of hammerhead sharks that frequent a spot only minutes away.

You are free to roam about the island and patronize the restaurants in the other two resorts and charge your bills to the resort you are staying at. My favourite food outlet on the island has to be the coffee-house at Kuramathi Village on the southern end. The *tandoori* chicken and the deliciously hot Indian curries are a must.

11. Nika Hotel (Kuda Folhudu)

No of rooms: 25 and 1 suite; Distance from airport: 68km (42½ miles); Price range: $$$$: Local agent: Nika Hotel office, 10 Fareedhee Magu, Malé. Tel: 32-5091, Fax: 32-5097

Cruising southwest from Kuramathi one arrives at Nika Hotel, on the northwestern tip of Ari Atoll. The helicopter transfer from Malé International Airport to Bodu Folodhu helipad takes 20 minutes, followed by a short *dhoni* ride to the resort.

Named after a local tree, Nika was first leased by an Italian architect who fell in love with Maldives in the early 1980s and built his dream home here. It was later converted into a small hotel before being renovated to its present structure. The island is luxuriantly green with coconut palms, screwpines and breadfruit. A huge amount of soil was imported from Sri Lanka for the planting of vegetables and fruits trees. You can be assured of fresh salads and freshly picked fruits at every meal here.

Total privacy and seclusion are top priorities for its 50 odd guests. For its high prices, you are accommodated in spacious bungalows, each 70sq m (750sq ft) in size. Well-camouflaged by thick foliage, each bungalow has its own little garden and a private stretch of beach to laze on. Built of coral and wood, the bungalows are built to resemble a shell;

Mega-sized rooms

Nika boasts private beaches for each of its 25 bungalows

the walls subtly embellished with breadfruit leaf designs. High ceilings, fans and the many open windows keep the rooms cool.

Much effort has been made to make Nika stand apart from the other luxury resorts, a fact appreciated by the wealthy Italians who come here. The buffet spread is superb, almost indulgent, with a wide selection of meat and fish dishes, pastas, salads, fruits and desserts. There is also a grill corner where you can have a steak done just the way you like it – something of a rarity in Maldives. A fine range of wines and champagne complement every meal.

An added bonus here is that if you are stranded at the airport because of a delayed arrival and missed the transfer, free accommodation is provided in a private guest-house in Malé till the next transfer to the resort. Also, when there is ample time before departure, guests are taken on a tour of Malé and given access to the guest-house to freshen up and rest before leaving.

12. Kuda Rah Island Resort

No of rooms: 30; Distance from airport: 96km (60 miles);
Price range: $$$; Local agent: 2/F, H Merry Side, Marine Drive,
Malé. Tel: 32-2335, Fax: 32-2335

Going by helicopter to Maafushivaru, and another 10 minutes by *dhoni*, you arrive at Kuda Rah, just across from Twin Island Resort on Maafushivaru island. This Mediterranean-style resort with its white-washed bungalows is managed by an Italian-Maldivian team and caters to a largely Italian and German clientele. The bungalows are spacious, and each is luxuriously furnished with two king-sized beds. Everything is of a grand scale here, down to the bathroom with its little garden. Besides the bath, there is an open-air shower.

Kuda Rah is kept immaculately clean and is beautifully land-scaped throughout, with lots of flowering plants and fruit trees. The frangipani, the emblem of Kuda Rah, permeates the islands with its heady scent. There is no lack of fresh fruits at your table. Instead of flower pots, cut tree-stumps are used to hold brightly-coloured flowers all over the island.

The attention given to the land also extends to the surrounding reef. Twice a day, it's feeding time for the many fishes around the lagoon, which probably explains the plethora of fishes swimming around the island. Kuda Rah has a rich

Greenery and flowers abound house reef that is home to a school of sting-rays, some of which are more than 2m (6½ft) across. Divers should know that the resort is home to one of four fully-staffed re-compression chambers in Maldives. In an attempt to protect the marine life around the island, Kuda Rah has banned waterskiing. But there's a whole list of alternatives – windsurfing, canoeing, diving and fishing – to keep you occupied.

Relaxing by Kuda Rah's fresh-water pool

Ten minutes by boat from Malé International Airport lies the capital island of Malé (pronounced Mah-lee). This is the geographical centre of Maldives, the focal point of all trade and commerce, and the site for all governmental and administrative affairs.

Malé is tiny for a capital city. For an island of only 1.8sq km (0.7sq mile), including the reclaimed land to the west, Malé houses 56,000 people, about 25 percent of the total population. Add to this the hundreds of people who come here each day for their separate needs, and the resulting close proximity and concentration of people can be almost unbearable under the hot Maldivian sun.

New construction sites are found everywhere in this rapidly ex-

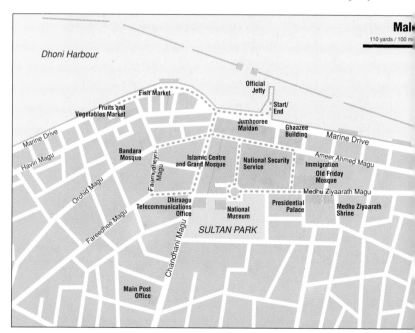

panding city. Although you can walk from one end to the other in 20 minutes, Malé has an excessively high number of cars, a result of a new affluence brought about by development. There are no traffic lights and the sight of cars and bicycles wildly criss-crossing one another can be daunting to the visitor.

While the average tourist is not likely to stay in Malé, most resorts organize a half-day trip to the capital for sightseeing and shopping. Nearby resorts in North and South Malé atolls can have as many as five excursions to Malé a week. Resorts normally avoid scheduling tours to the capital on Fridays, the official weekend, as most places of interest, offices and shops are closed. Rates for resort-organized excursions vary from US$18 to US$78, depending on the distance, the size of the tour group and whether lunch is provided. For resorts in the further-flung Ari Atoll, transfers to Malé can be costly and troublesome. If time allows, some try to include a trip to Malé for their guests on the day of departure.

Malé youth

If you do decide to spend a night or two on Malé while you shop around for resort packages with travel agents there, accommodation is available at a few hotels and guest houses. These are listed in the *Practical Information* section.

Malé City Tour

Most resort *dhonis* arrive at the inner harbour on the north side of Malé, near the **Official Jetty** which is strictly reserved for the President and high-ranking officials. Upon arrival, you are likely to be greeted by a gaggle of eager touts who will promise you the best bargains in nearby tourist shops. The situation can be a little annoying. It is best to refuse them politely and take a little time to see Malé before embarking on that sacred mission of souvenir-hunting for the folks back home.

Having stepped off the *dhoni*, you are on **Marine Drive**, (recently renamed Bodu Thakurufaanu Higun). This is the harbourfront road that circles most of the island. Since July 1993, many of the roads in Malé have been renamed but it is likely that 'Marine Drive' will continue to be used instead of the new tongue-twister. Don't worry too much about road names; the signboards are not easy to locate and when found, they are usually in the local script of *Thaana*, and of little help to the visitor. It is useful though to know that *magu* means a wide, unpaved coral street, *goalhi* is a narrow alley and a

A Divehi street sign

higun is a longer and wider alley. It is easy to get lost in the maze of similar looking houses and narrow streets, but Malé is small and you will not be lost for long. Fortunately, the few places of interest that you will visit are located near each other.

Directly in front of the jetty, across the green spread of **Jumhooree Maidan** or **Republic Park** is the **Islamic Centre**, whose main feature is the **Grand Mosque** with its golden dome so striking that you can see it from the sea as you approach Malé from the north. The Islamic Centre has a library, a conference hall and classrooms for religious studies. Opened in 1984, its prominence is a reflection of the role that Islam plays in the lives of the Maldivians.

The Grand Mosque (open daily 9am–5pm except during prayer times) with a capacity for 5,000 people is a stunning structure. Its interior is adorned with woodcarvings and Arabic calligraphy, all painstakingly done by Maldivian craftsmen. On Fridays, men dressed in their best congregate for the Friday prayers (*hukuru namaad*). The women pray at home or in separate mosques.

Bear in mind that this is a place of worship and therefore does not welcome hordes of gawking tourists, but should you wish to visit the mosque, it is advisable that you be accompanied by a Maldivian. Visitors are requested to dress appropriately and to observe strict silence.

As you come out of the

Grand Mosque with its eye-catching dome

mosque, you will find yourself on a little shady path called Iburaageemee Magu. The white wall facing you is part of the Headquarters of the National Security Service. Just a few metres to the right you will see a roundabout and the main road of Medhu Ziyaarath Magu. Across the road stands **Sultan Park** and the **National Museum** (open daily except Friday and public holidays, 9am–12pm and 3pm–6pm). The park surrounding the museum was once part of the sultan's palace. It is a quiet retreat from the hustle and bustle of Malé. Although much of the original palace was destroyed when the Sultanate was abolished, one remaining three-storey building has been converted to the National Museum.

There are a few caretakers who speak English at the museum. On display are a wide collection of clothes and ornaments used by past sultans and sultanas, handwritten *Quran* scriptures and interesting

pre-Islamic stone statues unearthed from many islands. Among these is the head of a Buddha image found on the island of Thoddu that dates back to pre-Islamic times. Another precious piece of antique is a 13th-century wooden panel inscribed with old scriptures.

One of the most amusing items is a motorbike near the entrance. This was used by one of the defending guards during

Pre-Islamic coral stone carving

the last coup and bears bullet holes fired by mercenaries.

To the right of the National Museum, a two-minute walk along the same road, is the **Mule-aage** or **Presidential Palace** with its ornate gates and security posts. This colonial-style building was originally designed by Ceylonese architects and commissioned by Sultan Mohammed Shamsuddeen III for his son in 1906. In May 1936, due to a political rift, the Sultan and his son were banished to the island of Fua Mulaku and the palace was declared as government property. It was used for government offices from 1942 to 1953, when it became the President's official residence. Today, the Presidential Palace is used to host state functions and to house visiting heads of states and other important visitors.

Adjoining the Presidential Palace at one corner is the **Medhu Ziyaarath**, a shrine built over the grave of Abu'al Barakath, the man responsible for bringing Islam to Maldives. Each morning, the shrine is kept fastidiously clean by an old man and every Friday, a white flag is hung as a mark of respect.

Opposite the Presidential Palace is the oldest and most beautiful mosque in Malé, the old **Friday Mosque** or **Hukuru Miskiiy**, built in 1656. The outside walls of the mosque

Gatekeeper, Medhu Ziyaarath

Door detail, Friday Mosque

are built with coral stones snugly fitted together without masonry, and the interior has old woodcarvings inscribed with Arabic writings which have been carefully preserved. In the garden within its compound are four wells for ritual ablutions and a sundial formerly used to calculate daily prayer times. Entry to the mosque is not permitted unless you have a special permit from the Department of Religious Affairs (Tel: 32-2266).

In the cemetery next to the Friday Mosque stand a number of elaborate tombstones erected in memory of past heroes like Sultan Ibrahim Iskandar I. An interesting feature of the tombstones is that those with pointed tops indicate the grave of a man and the rounded stones that of a woman. Outside the mosque stands an imposing white minaret. Built a year after the Friday Mosque was erected it was used for prayer calls in earlier times.

A block after turning left at the Friday Mosque, you find yourself on **Ameer Ahmed Magu** where most of the government offices are located. Hundreds of bicycles are parked alongside here. It is quite a novel sight in the afternoons when workers in their white shirts and ties take off *en masse* on their bicycles. Should you require any tourist information, the **Ministry of Tourism** is located

Return of fishing boats, Marine Drive

on the second floor of the blue **Ghaazee Building**. Turning left again and walking down Ameer Ahmed Magu, you pass the **Headquarters of the National Security Service** which you had a glimpse of earlier. Forget about taking pictures of the rifle-toting uniformed guard as it is prohibited.

Going past the Islamic Centre and right towards the waterfront, you arrive at Marine Drive again. The area that you will see to the

left is the market and goods receiving area – the busiest part of Malé. There is a perpetual confusion of people and activities at any hour of the day here as Malé is a big distribution centre which ships and receives goods to and from all the other islands.

If you should be in Malé during late afternoon, you will chance upon the highlight of the day – the return of the fishing boats. *Dhonies* spilling over with tuna, skipjack and bonito pull into the harbour just in front of the fish market

Malé fisherman

for the crew to unload their catch of the day. The **Fish Market** is dominated by men, and of course, snap-happy camera-toting tourists. This is not a place for the queasy as the air is always filled with the acrid smell of fresh blood and sweat.

Two blocks further down is the local market area. The sheltered area in front is where bundles of wood from the outer islands are brought in and traded. This wood, a precious commodity because of the lack of arable land, is used as firewood for cooking.

Just behind is the covered **fruits and vegetables market** where home-grown bananas, papayas, watermelons, pineapples,

The fruits and vegetables market

pumpkins, limes, pungent spices and stacks of leaves used for chewing with betelnut are sold.

Coconuts are in abundance, and if you are thirsty, a few *rufiyaa* will buy you some fresh coconut juice. The vendor will hack open the top of a young, green coconut, insert a straw and voila! After which, you are ready to turn back down Marine Drive and head for the main shopping area known as Singapore Bazaar in Malé.

Shopping

If you are a shopping fanatic, Maldives is definitely not the place for you. Tourist resorts usually have a boutique where you find the essentials and many of the same souvenir items that are available in Malé, but at much higher prices. Part of the fun of going on an excursion to Malé is to browse through the rows of colourful and quaint little shops in **Singapore Bazaar**, a nickname given to the sector bounded by Orchid Magu, Chandhani Magu and Fareedhee Magu.

Most of the items you see on sale here are imported from Sri Lanka, India, Indonesia or Thailand. There are few items which are Maldivian in origin because of the high labour costs here.

Most of the tourist shops in Malé are open from 9am to 11pm, but they close for a few minutes several times each day for prayers. If you are already inside, you can stay there. On Fridays, the shops are open only after 2pm. English is spoken at most shops, as is a smattering of German, Italian, French and Japanese. Bargaining is a must as there seems to be no fixed prices for the goods, and much depends on your bargaining skills and patience. You could save as much as 30 percent with a little haggling. As one signboard in a store boldly states: 'We are always open for discussion.'

What To Buy

Replica Dhonis

Among the local handicrafts are replica *dhonis* made of wood, coral or mother-of-pearl. These miniature *dhonis* can measure anything from 30cm (1ft) to 1m (3ft), complete with oars and sails. Among the most beautiful are those carved out of black coral and costing about US$500.

Singapore Bazaar

Black coral dhonis

The problem with these delicate items is handling and shipment. Bear in mind that many countries restrict the import of black coral and tortoiseshell for obvious reasons. Think carefully about the damage being done to the coral reefs before you make a purchase. **M Orchid Uffa** and **Gloria Maris** on Faamudheyri Magu have nice selections to choose from.

Shark's Teeth

Keen fishermen may like to pick up a set or two of shark's jaws as a memento of their trip. Having lost their bite, you will find displays of gaping jaws on the walls of numerous tourist shops. Recommended are **Schist** and **The Shop** along Fareedhee Magu. Costing between US$1 and US$250, these items make interesting conversation pieces.

The one that didn't get away

Coral Jewellery

A range of very pretty pink, red and black coral and shell jewellery can be found in almost all the tourist shops. The use of tortoiseshell is steadily decreasing because of a heightened awareness of the environment, but you can still find it here in ornamental forms. A fine display of jewellery items can be found at **Glamour Souvenirs** on Chandhani Magu.

Ethnic Jewellery

If coral ornaments go against your better judgement, there are nice collections of old silver and antique jewellery from India and Sri Lanka in many of the shops. Check around for the best prices and selections.

Reed Mats

Another local handicraft item worth considering are the reed mats or *tunda kunna* with their interesting black and brown motifs. These mats are naturally dyed and are often used as prayer mats and bed covers by the locals. The best of these mats come from the Gaddu and Fiyori islands in Huvadu Atoll.

Lacquerware

Perhaps the most popular souvenir from Maldives is the lacquerware known as *lielaa jehun* from the island of Thulhaadhu in Baa Atoll. Traditionally made from local wood, the lacquerware is crafted into items such as walking sticks, boxes, trays and vases. The most impressive are the large circular dishes with elaborate designs on their lids used for festive occasions. If you have visited the National Museum at Malé, you would have seen many fine examples used for royal functions in the past. Handpainted and carved with yellow, red and black floral patterns, *lielaa jehun* products can be found decorating the shelves of many Maldivian households. **Gloria Maris**, on the corner of Fareedhee and Faamudheyri Magu, has a nice collection of lacquerware, from small boxes to large, intricately-detailed pieces. Prices range from US$15–US$150.

Clothes

T-shirts are one of the best bargains in Malé. Some shops even custom-make designs to your specifications. Apart from stores selling T-shirts, singlets and assorted beachwear proclaiming 'Maldives' in day-glo colours, **Lemon**, a little shop along Chandhani Magu is a real gem. Run by a Maldivian and his Japanese wife, Lemon carries an assortment of colourful T-shirts embossed with designs such as coconut trees, fishes, *dhonis* and sails. Though more expensive and prices are fixed, the T-shirts are of better quality and the designs unique.

The *batik* you see at the stores is not Maldivian but Indonesian. The Maldives does produce a traditional brown and cream cloth known as *feli*, but these are very difficult to find. If you wish to buy some *batik*, check out **Bamboo**, one of the first few shops on Chandhani Magu. This store also carries a good range of leather bags of reasonable quality and prices. Another shop which specializes in *batik* is the **Royal Arts** on Orchid Magu.

If the heat should get to you – and it surely will – you can probably find all that you want in the cool comfort of **Najaah Artpalace**, which occupies the first and second floors of MHA Building, at the junction of Chandhani Magu and Orchid Magu. This is the largest and most complete of all the shops. Besides the above items, the shop also has a good collection of postcards and books on Maldives.

There are also a number of sundry shops along Orchid Magu and Chandhani Magu where you can find essentials such as soap, shampoo and toothpaste. For a wider selection, check out **People's Choice**, a large supermarket behind the Customs' Office near the western end of Malé. This is where many expatriates do their shopping.

Eating Out

One of the most common complaints among visitors at resorts is the amount of fish served at mealtimes. Bear in mind that fish is the staple food for the locals – the Maldivian dried fish can be cooked an umpteen number of ways – and almost everything else is imported from neighbouring countries. To be fair, the food served at most resorts is above average and usually a choice between a Western menu and a local curry and rice meal is offered. An international buffet is often part of the standard offering to cater to the varied tastes of the many nationalities. A wide range of alcohol and beer are sold at the bars in the resorts though this is prohibited on all locally inhabited islands and even in Malé.

Apart from the familiar curried fish and rice, few tourists ever venture at trying genuine Maldivian fare. Excursions to Malé are usually scheduled such that guests are back at the resorts for the main meals of the day, but after a week of endless buffets, resort food can get a little monotonous. For the curious, an excursion to Malé could serve as an eye-opener into discovering Maldivian cuisine.

Maldivian Food

Stepping into a local teahouse to savour a Maldivian meal with the locals can be a novel experience. On almost every street, you will find a teahouse close by. Tea-time in the Maldives, you will find, is very flexible and stretches from morning to midnight.

The teahouse, like the fish market, is the domain of men: women are rarely seen. Each time I've sat down on a long wooden bench found at

An array of teahouse treats

any one of the raucous teahouses, the men will politely shift away. You will find well-dressed office workers having their meals along-side *sarong*-clad fishermen. Many of the teahouses are open for breakfast early in the morning and close at about midnight. In the evening, they become popular hangouts for young Maldivians since nightlife and entertainment is practically non-existent in Malé.

There are no menus in the teahouses. An assortment of short eats or *hedhikaa* are laid out on every table in small portions. You are only charged for what you consume, though it always bemuses me how the waiter remembers what is eaten and by whom. For a start, if you plan to eat with your hands like the locals, always use the right hand to pick at the food and the left to handle cutlery.

For a few *rufiyaa* one can have a hearty meal, washed down by a cup of very sweet tea with milk. If you find the tea too sweet, tell the waiter to hold the sugar. Most of the snacks are made of a mix-

ture of fish, meat, co-conut, wheat and rice flours, and then deep-fried. Many of these are hot and spicy, like *kuli bokibaa*, a spicy fish cake with garlic and chillies and *gulg*, a round fish roll mixed with coconut and onion. There is also *bajiya*, made of fish and onions wrapped into trian-gular shapes, and *foni bakibaa*, a baked pas-try with fried onions.

A Malé teahouse scene

Another savoury snack is *bis keemiya* a combination of cabbage, onions and eggs. For the sweet-toothed, there is *folhi*, a flour and sugar mixture. *Donkeo kajuru* are fried banana-flavoured balls and *keku* is a sweet fluffy cake. For lunch and dinner, there is always a separate table on which dishes of curried fish, vegetables and rice are placed to supplement the variety of snacks. Popular among the locals is the plain flat bread or *roshi*, torn into small pieces and dipped into curries.

Although most teahouses serve almost identical food, my personal favourite is **Market Hotel**, situated above the Fish Market where you can watch *dhonis* coming in and the busy street below. **The Queen of the Night**, on Marine Drive near the Nasandhura Palace Hotel, prepares some of the most fragrant fried chicken I've tried. For some tasty fried noodles and snacks, look out for **Evening Glory** on Majeedhee Magu. Among the locals, **Majeedhee Ufaa**, at the junction of Majeedhee Magu and Chandhani Magu, and **Hotel Dhanbuma** on Faamudheyri Magu are very popular.

Restaurants in Malé

If eating in a local teahouse is not exactly your cup of tea, there are several restaurants serving non-Maldivian food in Malé. Compared to the local teahouses where you can have a meal for about Rf20, the restaurants will seem like a costly affair.

The average price range for a meal for two persons is as follows:

Inexpensive = less than US$15
Moderate = US$15–US$30
Expensive = US$30–US$45

PARK VIEW RESTUARANT
Chandhani Magu
Tel: 32-8106
Considered to be the most expensive in the city, the setting is rather posh by Malé standards. The menu offers a wide selection from Continental, Indian and Chinese cuisines. Open daily 11am–midnight; Fridays, dinner only. *Expensive*

ATHMAA PALACE RESTAURANT
Majeedhee Magu
Tel: 31-3118
Serves tasty Chinese and Indian cuisine with a nice selection of vegetarian dishes in a very pleasant setting. Open daily 11am–3pm and 7pm–11pm. *Moderate*

TRENDS
Nasandhura Palace Hotel
Marine Drive
Tel: 32-2280
A pleasant open-air restaurant serving a variety of Western and Asian dishes. Open daily 9.30am–1am. *Moderate*

DRAGON RESTAURANT
Marine Drive and Burevi Magu, Henveiru
Tel: 32-2009
One of the most popular among the expatriate community in Malé. Serves a good selection of Thai dishes despite the Chinese-sounding name. Open daily 11.30am–2.30pm and 7pm–11pm. Closed on the last Friday of the month. *Moderate*

SLICE
Faamudheyri Magu
Tel: 32-0566
Conveniently located in the Singapore Bazaar, this is a nice little joint for fish and chips or a hamburger and milkshake if you hunger for food from back home. Open daily from about 8.30am–midnight. *Inexpensive*

GROUND SIX RESTAURANT
Relax Inn
Ameer Ahmed Magu
Tel: 31-4531
Located on the top floor of the Relax Inn Hotel, this restaurant serves Western and Asian cuisine prepared by a Sri Lankan chef. Has a lovely view of the harbour and the Grand Mosque. Open daily 7am–10am, noon–2pm and 7pm–1pm. *Moderate*

TWIN PEAKS RESTAURANT
Orchid Magu
Tel: 32-7830
Menu of Western and Asian dishes, from *tempura* to steak and fries here. Open daily 10am–11pm; Fridays, dinner only. *Moderate*

Diving

Maldives is one of those rare destinations that offer excellent diving opportunities for all levels, from novice to expert. Instruction is available to meet every need, from resort courses for those taking the plunge for the first time to advanced and speciality courses for experienced divers. For novices, there are flat fields of soft corals, gentle slopes and dense aggregations of fishes. For experienced divers there are opportunities for drift diving and night diving, and there are plenty of steep walls, pinnacles and caverns to explore. There is also a chance to do a wreck dive. And for the group in between, there is an endless variety of reefs just waiting to be explored.

Dynamite fishing is unknown in Maldives; the local fisherman go offshore for tuna, and spear-fishing was outlawed in the mid-70s. Warm, clear waters and an abundance of healthy coral reefs attract an astonishing array of fishes and other marine life.

Good diving is everywhere in Maldives – as close as the beach at your resort, or as far as the farthest atoll from Malé. You will not have to take long boat trips in order to reach good dive sites. As many of the 200,000 plus visitors who flock to these islands each year make it their major recreation, most resorts operate diving schools. These are run by dive base operators from Sub-Aqua, Inter-Aqua, EuroDivers, Manta Reisen, Club Med, Club Vacanze and other well-known groups.

A rare encounter with a leopard moray eel

A school of squirrelfish

Most resorts have a house reef that you can access from the beach. Some are true reefs, others are scattered coral heads on a sandy bottom. **Ellaidhoo** is reputed to have the best house reef; some of the other good ones are at **Bandos**, **Vadu**, **Embudhu Village**, **Giraavaru**, **Helengeli**, **Baros**, **Kuda Rah** and **Twin Island (Maafushivaru)**. These are only a few of the better house reefs, there are many others. In general, most resorts are surrounded by very nice little reefs. If you want to do a lot of beach diving, check beforehand that the resort you have chosen has an accessible house reef. For those wishing to venture farther afield, live-aboard yacht-*dhonis* run dive safaris to some of the more remote reefs.

If you have never dived before and you are in good health, short resort courses are available, as are certification, speciality and advanced courses. Be sure to bring along your diving certification card (C-card) and your log book because all reputable dive operators will ask to see them. If you have not dived recently, you may be asked to do a checkout dive, or at least an easy first dive so that the divemaster can see how comfortable you are in the water. Given the remote location of Maldives and the lack of sophisticated

Resort diving, Rihiveli

medical treatment available, this extra precaution is well worth the small inconvenience it may cause anyone.

Maldivian Reefs

Maldives, a double strand of atolls covering over 90,000sq km (34,750sq miles) of the Indian Ocean, forms the central part of the volcanic Laccadives-Chagos Ridge. Its 26 atolls include Huvadhoo, one of the largest atolls in the world.

Atolls are generally believed to form when ancient volcanoes surrounded by fringing reefs subside into the ocean. As the volcanic land mass slowly sinks, the coral reef around the edges continues to build up. This process continues until the volcano is completely submerged and only the built-up coral ring, or atoll, remains. Natural breaks in the reef form the passes used by boats to move in and out of the atolls. Over time, sand and coral debris build up on the reef and form low-lying islands. The process of atoll formation takes millions of years and was first recognized by Charles Darwin in the 1830s. His theory of atoll formation has been substantiated by a number of ocean drilling and test bore samples taken during the last 50 years.

Each atoll, speckled with small islands, encircles a large lagoon. The lagoons, ranging in depth from 40–90m (130–300ft), are dotted with coral heads, shallow reefs and thilas – deeper submerged reefs that rise from the sandy bottom. The calm waters inside the lagoons provide favourable conditions for the formation of large areas of branching and reef-building corals that are home to many of the 900 or so species of fish found here. If you wish to identify the fishes you see, check with your resort boutique for a series of fish identification books by Dr R C Anderson, a resident marine biologist.

Some 900 species of fish thrive here

Maldives has many faros, or ring-like submerged reefs, inside the atolls. These formations are not unique, but the fact that they occur here with such frequency is. Faros near the outer edges of the atolls are longer, and some are open at one end like a horseshoe rather than a ring, but both rise from the atoll floor and have sandy bottoms, forming lagoons within lagoons. Faro lagoons are typically shallow, less than 6m (20ft) deep, but some are as deep as 40m (130ft).

Each island is fringed by its own 'house reef', which provides opportunities for easy beach diving at many of the resort islands. Visibility inside the lagoons can vary but it is generally quite good.

There are passes in the lagoons separating the outer reef sections, and channels outside the lagoons separating the atolls. Both have strong currents supporting a wide variety of marine life and often have steep sides pockmarked with ledges and overhangs which shelter scores of reef fishes, lobsters, shrimps and crabs. The channels

and some of the passes are known for the variety of pelagic fishes like rays and sharks to be found, and for their exciting drift dives. In depth, the passes vary from quite shallow to very deep, while channels are deeper, with depths exceeding 200m (650ft).

The outer walls along the sides of the atolls drop off sharply to much greater depths, where the surrounding waters can be 1,000 –3,000m (3,280–9,850ft) deep. There are a few true vertical reef walls in Maldives, and although most of the outer reefs have steep slopes, there are some places where the drop-off is gradual.

The water outside the atolls is clear and the marine life is intense in quantity and colour, although some of the reefs along the western edge of North and South Malé atolls have been affected by the crown-of-thorns starfish which feed on coral polyps and can cause extensive damage to the reefs.

When to Dive

The very best time to dive is between January and April when the seas are calm, the skies are sunny, and the water is at its clearest, with visibility well over 30m (100ft). Beginning in late August and continuing through October, whales are seen in the channel at the southern tip of Ari Atoll. But if you want to see manta rays, and possibly a whale shark, the best time to dive in North or South Malé atolls is August through November when the waters are rich with plankton; in Ari Atoll, February through April are the best months for seeing them. Diving is good all year but rain, wind and

---

Manta Rays and Whale Sharks

Depending on the season, you may chance upon manta rays, and less often, whales or whale sharks. Reaching a length of 14m (45ft) or more, the whale shark is the world's largest fish. Unlike its more notorious relatives, this shark is a plankton eater and can be seen swimming slowly, often with its mouth agape, straining tiny organisms from the water. Manta rays – huge fish that seem to fly through the water – also feed on plankton. With a wingspan that can exceed 6m (20ft), manta rays are an awesome presence when encountered. Far removed from Captain Nemo's leviathans of the deep, these giants are not dangerous but curious, and if not harassed, will sometimes glide over to a group of divers for a closer look before flying off into the deep blue.

A whale shark seen off Ari Atoll

rough sea conditions occur more often during the southwest monsoon season (June–August), and can make getting to some dive sites difficult, if not impossible.

During this time the visibility can vary, occasionally dropping to as low as 10m (33ft). The weather is said to run in two-week cycles, but this is not a hard and fast rule as many say the weather pattern is changing. Winds from the northeast in December and January sometimes make it difficult to reach the best dive sites on the outer eastern side of the atolls, but there are always protected areas inside the lagoon and on the sheltered side of the passes where you can dive.

Visibility often exceeds 30m (100ft) and the water temperature is a very comfortable 27°–30°C (80°–86°F), making heavy wetsuits unnecessary, although you will be more comfortable with a lightweight suit.

Maldivian Diving Rules

The Maldivian government has developed some diving regulations which they believe will help to make diving a safer sport. Decompression diving is forbidden, spear-fishing is illegal and dives deeper than 30m (100ft) are discouraged. Also, buoyancy compensators (BCs) are a must.

Some dive operations have their own diving rules as well. These usually include a check-out dive: once the instructor is satisfied you are comfortable in the water, you are free to dive without a guide and usually do not have to follow the group. Some resorts further ask that on boat dives you surface within one hour or with 50 bar (750 psi) remaining in your tank, whichever comes first. This rule varies, depending on the dive operation and the number and skill of the divers on board. The taking of corals and other marine life is discouraged, as is solo diving.

Shark feeding has fallen into disfavour of late and is not done on a regular basis. Check with your dive operator for current information on shark feeding.

BCS are compulsory

Resort Diving

Resort dive operations typically offer daily morning and afternoon boat dives at dive sites less than an hour away; night dives are available on request at most resorts. Resorts with accessible house reefs usually offer unlimited beach diving packages. Some resorts, like Bandos and Ellaidhoo, offer round-the-clock beach diving. Boat dives are made from local *dhonis*, large and roomy enough to accommodate divers and all their equipment, and they are covered to offer protection from the sun. These boats usually accommodate between four and 20 divers. All-day excursions to remote dive sites are regularly organized and include two boat dives, and either a packed lunch or a barbecue on an uninhabited island. Sometimes, a visit to another resort is included.

Resort diving packages: You can get a variety of diving packages at reduced rates; a good idea if you plan to dive for several days. Unlimited diving packages usually include two boat dives a day and unlimited beach diving on the house reef. I recommend this option if your resort has a good house reef, and if you want to do more than two dives a day. The boat fee is often charged separately, but some resorts offer a discount if you purchase one of their diving packages. Some scuba diving is included in the price of a stay at Club Med and at Club Vacanze. On the average, a one-dive package will set you back US$25, six dives US$131, 10 dives US$222 and six days of unlimited diving about US$226. The boat fee averages from US$9 for one trip to US$15 for two trips per person.

Getting a feel of the water

Prices for diving packages include tanks and weight belts only, but resort dive shops have all types of rental equipment – subject to availability. Some also have dive computers and underwater cameras and strobes for rent. However, not all dive operations rent wetsuits. Equipment rental averages about US$5 a day for full scuba gear. Individual pieces rent for US$2 per day and up.

Introductory dive: If you've never dived before, you should try an introductory dive or a resort course. These courses are an introduction to scuba diving, and are designed to get you into the water under the close supervision of a dive instructor so you can see what you have been missing. The introductory dive is just that – a short lecture and demonstration followed by a beach dive in the resort lagoon and on the house reef. This introduction is short, less than half a day, and will help you decide if you would like to pursue the sport. Most resorts offer introductory dives for about US$32, equipment included. If you decide to do a certification course, some resorts will deduct the cost of the introductory dive from the certification course.

Resort course: These are offered by some, but not all, resorts. These courses are longer than the introductory class and include between three and six closely-supervised dives. The first three dives are

A classroom session

usually done in the lagoon and on the house reef; some diving schools then allow boat dives at their discretion. Prices for resort courses vary from US$110 for a three-day, three-dive course to US$250 for a six-day, six-dive course. All equipment is included, but the boat fee is often charged separately.

Some schools offer a certificate and a log book for participating in a resort course, but do remember that this is not a certification for diving and will not be honoured anywhere else in the world should you want to go diving again. The resort course is meant to serve as an introduction to scuba diving, and if you enjoyed it, your next step is to take a certification course leading to the C-card.

C-Card: The major certifying agencies here are PADI, NAUI and CMAS. Other certifications are available but on a smaller scale. The dive schools have at least one dive instructor, and depending on the resort and the instructors available, courses can be given in all the major European languages and Japanese. You will be asked to complete a medical questionaire before enrolling in the course. The cost for a standard open water certification course is about US$400 (equipment included); an advanced course is about US$200 and includes instruction on night diving, search and recovery, and underwater navigation. Be sure to check with the dive school to see if boat fees are included in the price.

Helicopter Diving

If you are looking for a diving package that is out of the ordinary, Hummingbird Helicopters operate one-day diving adventures from Malé International Airport. Arriving at Ari Beach or Kandolodhu in Ari Atoll, diving *dhonis* take you to the first dive site, then return you to the beach for a barbecue lunch and some time to relax in the sun. The second dive is a short boat ride away before you are whisked back to Malé. The trips leave at 9am and return by 5pm. The all-inclusive cost is US$199.

En-route to diving

Dive safari boat MV *Keema*

Dive Safaris

One- and two-week dive safaris are available for those who do not want to be tied to a land-based operation. All safaris start and end in Malé, and typically visit Ari or Baa atoll on one-week trips, or both on two-week excursions; some boats combine visits to South Malé and Felidu atolls. Most safari tours are flexible and companies can tailor a specific plan to meet the needs of your group. During the high season from January through April, safari boats are usually full and it is best to book your reservation in advance. Note: some boats require a minimum number of divers.

Safari boats are fully equipped yacht-*dhonis* ranging in length from 12–20m (40–65ft) with beams of 4–6m (13–20ft). They can accommodate between two and 14 passengers. A diving *dhoni* accompanies each dive safari boat, storing the compressor, tanks and other equipment, and ferrying divers to and from the dive sites.

A diving dhoni

Two dives a day, interspersed with visits to resorts and fishing villages is the norm, but arrangements can be made in advance to do more diving. Dive safaris run US$60–US$70 per person per day (full board), plus diving fees of US$300–US$500 for 12 dives. The diving fee includes the boat charge, tanks, weights, air fills and the services of a dive-master. Safari boats can be booked through Voyages Maldives (Tel: 32-3019, Fax: 32-5336) and Phoenix Travels Pvt Ltd (Tel: 32-3181, Fax: 32-5499). These are the two largest dive safari operators in Malé. Club Vacanze has its own diving safari boat in Maldives which you can book through any Club Vacanze office overseas.

The MV *Keema*, operated by Rob Bryning and Samantha Harwood for the past three years, is set up specifically for diving. This modified 25-m (80-ft) yacht-*dhoni* takes 12 people in six twin cabins.

She sails on regularly scheduled departure dates from August through May. Most divers do three dives a day; night dives are optional. Bryning and Harwood have been diving in Maldives for four years and know how to locate some terrific dive sites. Diving equipment is available for rent, as is underwater photography gear: two video cameras, strobes and Nikonos cameras. The *Keema* has video monitors for viewing your daily footage, as well as on-board E-6 processing for your slides. There is fresh water for rinsing cameras and for showers. Although the *Keema* caters for experienced divers, non-divers are welcome. However, diving instruction is not available on board. The booking agent in Europe for the *Keema* is in UK: Maldives Scuba Tours Ltd (Tel: 44-449-766116, Fax: 44-449-766069).

Drift Diving

Strong currents provide an opportunity for excellent drift dives in the many passes and channels in and between the atolls. As you move down the reef, look for schools of fishes hanging in mid-water and for schools of jacks swimming against the current. A quick glance at the reef as you drift by will tell you just how swiftly the current is moving. Extend your arms out from your sides, lean forward and fly over the reef. Be on the lookout for manta rays feeding in the current; look down as you fly over stately coral trees crowned with feather stars; wave at the passing fishes. You will find it hard to see everything as the reef becomes a smear of bright colours as you glide past. When it is time to ascend, break the surface and you will see your diving *dhoni* nearby; signal and it will come pick you up.

Night Diving

Night dives are often rewarding because of the likelihood of seeing new and different marine life. Fish photography is less difficult at night because fishes in their resting state can be approached more easily than during sunlight hours.

As the sun goes down, the reef takes on a different look as familiar reef fishes switch into their nighttime modes. Wrasses cover themselves with sand, butterflyfishes take on a darker night colouration and snuggle up to coral heads, small fishes

A parrotfish resting at night

take shelter in crevices and holes, and parrotfishes surround themselves with protective mucus bags.

When the retreat is complete, the nocturnal animals emerge. Cup corals colour the reef walls with bright yellow and orange polyps while sea cucumbers lumber across the sand between sea pens. Sweep the reef with your dive light and you will spot soldierfish darting about in their deep red night colours. Examine soft tree corals to find small crabs decorated with bits of sponges and corals for camouflage. Look around for feather stars – curled up during the day, they extend their arms at night to feed. If you dive in the right area, this is the time for the flashlight fishes to appear; turn off your dive light and you may see them winking in the dark.

To see these extraordinary fishes, find a place near the top of a cavern or recess, turn off all lights and wait. In a few minutes you will see flashing green lights; first one, then two, then several, and soon a sea of them. If you want to photograph these unique fishes, use a 1:4 framer with a Nikonos; if using a housed camera, focus on the pocket of light – either way it is not easy and patience is a must.

Flashlight Fish

An intriguing sight on some night dives are the flashing green lights belonging to the elusive flashlight fish, *Photoblepharon steinitzi*. Found in caverns on moonless nights, this small (10–12cm/4–5in) dark fish collects bioluminescent bacteria in a special pouch-like organ located just under each eye. When the pouch is exposed it shows up as a bright green light. The flashlight fish can turn the light on or off at will by covering and uncovering the organ with a flap of skin. The luminous organs are thought to be used to communicate with other flashlight fishes, to see and attract prey, and to confuse predators.

Underwater Photography

Plenty of sunshine and fine visibility provide unlimited opportuni-

ties for the underwater photographer. Because the subjects range from very small to very large, you should bring close-up and wide-angle equipment with you. Either way you are sure to find something interesting to capture on film. If you have never tried underwater photography, this is a great place to learn by renting a camera.

The power supply for charging strobes is 220V. If your strobe takes regular batteries you should bring an ample supply from home. Batteries are available at resorts, but they are

Photographing the undersea world

expensive and the ones that you need may not always be available.

Kodak and Fuji films are generally available at the resorts; Kodak Underwater Ektachrome is available in Malé and at some of the resorts. Film prices are high so it is best to bring a supply from home. Print film and all slide films except Kodachrome can be developed and returned to you within a few hours, or a few days, depending on your location. The following resorts do in-house slide processing (E-6): Club Med, Bandos, Madoogale, Olhuveli, Ellaidhoo, Kuredhoo and Alimatha. Bandos also does print processing. Some dive operations do E-6 processing independently, depending on staff expertise and demand.

Underwater Hazards

It is easy to get caught up in the beauty of the underwater world and forget about problems associated with diving. In general, diving in Maldives is not hazardous, but some things are worth noting. Always listen to your dive guide – he or she knows the area and the water conditions better than you do. Always use your good judgment and err on the side of safety. There are very strong currents in some areas and it is easy to become separated from the group. If you get caught in a current, swim across it – not against it – to calmer water. Some resorts, but not all, provide dive sausages (a long inflatable tube that fits into a BC pocket) for their divers so they can easily be seen by the boat operator at the end of a dive. Most dive shops stock these inexpensive safety devices, so pick one up before you leave home.

Occasionally, you will see a sea urchin or crown-of-thorns starfish on the reef. Try not to touch them. Their spines carry some venom, and although their stings are seldom serious, they can cause a certain amount of discomfort. Remember, once you have been been pricked, you will not be able to remove the brittle spines and will have to wait for your body to dissolve them naturally.

You may come across a well-camouflaged scorpionfish, or more rarely, a stonefish. Don't bother them and they won't bother you. If you spot a lionfish, keep your distance as along the length of its spectacular plume-like fins are a series of poisonous glands. If you are accidentally stung by one of these creatures, immediately immerse the wound and the surrounding areas in hot water – as hot as you can stand it. Although the heat will inactivate the venom, you should also seek medical attention.

Wetsuits are unnecessary for warmth here, but they can make diving a bit more comfortable by protecting you from accidental coral abrasions and the sting of unseen hydroids or stinging plankton. A small bottle of Stingose from your local dive shop quickly neutralizes painful hydroid stings. Vinegar and wet tea bags may be used but they are less effective remedies.

The combination of sun and sea increases your risk of sunburn. Be sure to use a good sun block before and after each dive – even when the

Lionfish: spectacular but poisonous

dive site is only a short boat ride away. And don't forget a hat and sunglasses.

One final note of caution: make an extra effort to monitor your depth gauge or dive computer regularly during your dives. Because the water is so clear, it is easy to exceed your planned depth limit without realizing it.

Dive operators are required to carry a supply of oxygen on the diving *dhoni* for use in the event of emergencies. Dive operations normally have enough oxygen available to support someone until they can get to a recompression chamber.

At present, there are four fully-staffed recompression chambers in Maldives – at Club Med and Bandos in North Malé atoll, Kuda Rah in Ari Atoll and Alimatha in Felidu Atoll. There are several other recompression chambers in Ari Atoll, but they are not staffed on a full-time basis. In an emergency, you can charter a helicopter for transfer to a chamber that is out of your *dhoni* or speedboat range.

– *Denise Tackett*

Keep an eye on the air level

Dive Sites

There are hundreds of places to dive in Maldives but only some highlights can be described here. One dive operator may frequent the same dive sites as another, but they may know the sites by different names. Some reefs, like the famous Banana Reef, are widely known by only one name. To further confuse things, some reef names are repeated in different areas. For example, there are at least four Manta Points and probably more. Keep in mind

A cleaner wrasse feeding off an oriental sweetlips

that these sites represent Maldivian diving in general – sites like these (excluding the wrecks) can be found in many locations here. And there are many equally beautiful unnamed sites. Please refer to IFC and page 1 maps for the following dive locations.

North Malé Atoll

Banana Reef: Rises to within a couple of metres of the surface at its northeastern tip, then drops straight down to 15m (50ft), revealing a series of overhangs housing numerous fish cleaning stations. Look for striped cleaner wrasses, gobies and shrimps that hover near the back walls of the overhangs, waiting patiently for their next customer.

If you swim east, to the tip of the reef, you can often see a large school of bannerfish just off the point. From the reef overhangs, turn and look out to the huge boulders that rise from the depths a few metres away. These pinnacles are the home of the larger fishes – oriental sweetlips, groupers and big eyes. They gather in groups, motionless in the currents, or they sidle up to the reef, surrounded by hundreds of bright orange fairy basslets. This section of the reef is absolutely filled with fishes.

About 45m (150ft) farther west along the reef is a big cavern with walls lined with night-blooming cup corals. Spend a few minutes exploring and you will see small lobsters peeking out from their holes in the reef and waving their antennae-like streamers. Colourful sponges and reef fishes add to the festive atmosphere of this reef. This is an excellent reef for wide-angle and close-up photography.

Poodle's Place: Takes its name from an exposed rock, shaped like a poodle, that marks the dive site. At 10m (33ft), the water is filled with brightly coloured fishes that dart in and out amongst

Fish Cleaning Stations

The healthy fish life found on Maldivian reefs is due in part to the abundance of cleaner fish and shrimps found here. These cleaners have a mutually beneficial relationship with the fishes they clean. They remove dead and diseased tissue, as well as tiny parasitic crustaceans from their customers in exchange for a free meal.

The cleaner you will most often see here is the blue-streak cleaner wrasse, *Labroides dimidiatus*. This small brightly-coloured fish dances around its territory, often a small coral head, advertising its services. Several species of cleaner shrimps occupy reef crevices and attract customers by waving their long white antennae.

When a fish glides into a cleaning station, the cleaner immediately begins its work while the fish remains motionless, sometimes in a headstand, often changing colour during the cleaning process. Fishes, including moray eels, open their mouths wide, allowing cleaners to work inside with no fear of being devoured.

Cleaning stations are popular and you will see fishes queuing at busy stations. Studies have shown that fish life on reefs deteriorate quickly if the cleaners are removed.

the table corals and smaller coral heads. Just over the edge you may see a school of unicorn fish, frequent visitors to this reef.

As you descend, notice the series of cleaning stations along the reef. Keep moving down the reef face as it drops steeply to 20m (66ft) where you will find the top of a large cavern. At 30m (100ft) on the cavern floor are black corals, sea fans, decorated sponges and sea whips. Take a closer look at the sea whips and try to find

A banded cleaner shrimp

the tiny sea whip gobies amongst the polyps. Swim over to the back wall for a better look at the soldierfishes that fill the recesses of the cavern by day.

Hans' Place: Located a bit farther west, in a recess on the same reef as Poodle's Place, this is a great spot for taking photos of fish cleaning stations. This is a steep reef slope with a series of overhangs beginning at 6m (20ft). The overhangs are covered with small sea fans and it seems as if every recess in the reef is a cleaning station. Big red squirrelfish and oriental sweetlips gather in groups under the overhangs. Look for a school of blue triggerfish grazing along the reef and for a group of grey snappers swimming just off the reef. Small white-tip reef sharks are sometimes seen here.

Rainbow Reef: A small reef on the east side of Malé atoll, it is known for its caverns and canyons covered with soft corals and filled with fishes, including jacks and Napolean wrasses. Sometimes sharks are seen in this area.

Manta Point: Takes its name from the giant manta rays that frequent this area. The best photos here are shot by using a wide-angle (15–20mm) lens. Most of the action is on the reef at 15m (50ft). Located near the entrance to a pass that carries an abundance of plankton, the larger coral heads serve as cleaning stations for the manta rays who glide in from the deep and linger just over the reef top while dozens of small fishes pick the parasites from them. This is only one of several manta points in Maldives.

Lion's Head: Found along the south side of the atoll, this is a great place for watching sharks. Shark feeding sometimes takes place at this location even though it is not necessary to offer food to attract them. At 15m (50ft) is an open area in front of a big cavern

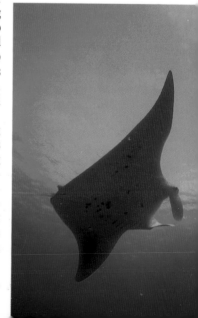

A manta in motion

that makes a nice arena for shark-watching divers. Grey reef sharks appear out of nowhere and swim to the edge of the reef where you can get a closer look at them. Elsewhere there are large groupers and snappers to be found along with the more familiar reef fishes. The cavern is filled with soldierfishes and small sea fans.

Old Shark Point: Another nice dive site. The area gradually slopes down to 15m (50ft), turning into a series of canyons and pinnacles that shelter all sorts of invertebrates and fishes. There is a big mantis shrimp here – reputed to be at least 10 years old – in a burrow that is protected by a circle of rocks. Schools of pelagic fishes swim just off the reef, large parrotfishes and Napolean wrasses cruise through the canyons and angelfish hug the reef. Look

for a variety of undulating flatworms here too. An excellent spot for wide-angle and macro photography.

Wreck of the Victory: Maldives' best wreck dive sits in 37m (120ft) of water at the southern tip of Hulhule, the airport island. The *Victory* was a cargo vessel from Singapore that sunk in 1981 when she hit the reef while entering the atoll at midnight. She went down with a cargo of cas-

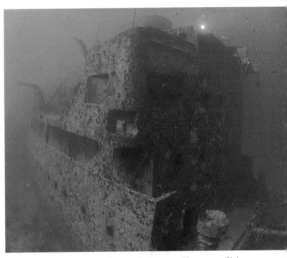
The Victory is in excellent condition

sette tapes and small appliances. Most of the valuable cargo was removed without delay but remnants can be seen in the ship's holds and strewn about in the surrounding sand.

The 62-m (203-ft) long *Victory*, with its superstructure intact, is in excellent condition and sits upright on a sandy bottom. The anchor chain is still hanging from the port bow, suspending the anchor just above the sand. Explore the main deck with its two open cargo holds, masts forward and amidships, and two large booms lying across the deck. A family of batfish often linger near the top of the forward mast. Along the deck look for cylinders and reels of line.

At 20m (65ft), at the stern of the ship, is the bridge; a great place to stop and watch the passing schools of snappers and jacks. Once on the bridge you will find the telegraph intact, but the ship's wheel, radio and other bridge instruments are missing. Survey the cabins below and look for the large ceramic bath and several toilets. Along both sides of the bridge are lifeboat davits hanging down, but no lifeboats. Behind the bridge is the ship's funnel and a

Colourful sea sponge

small, rear deck with several large bollards. As you swim the length of the ship, notice the variety of fishes swimming in and out of the nooks and crannies. Corals, sponges, anemones and other clusters of marine life have formed small colonies along the length of the ship.

South Malé Atoll

Guradu Channel: A photographer's paradise. The south side of the channel drops off sharply to 25m (82ft), then gradually slopes down to 46m (150ft) or so before dropping off steeply to a sandy bottom. Occasional strong currents make for exciting drift dives here. The almost vertical wall is pitted with small caverns and ledges and the overhangs are filled with fishes and lush soft coral growth. Electric blue and pink tree corals with colours so vivid they seem to be lit from within line the reef walls. Even sponges, normally inconspicuous, seem to vie for attention here with their bright blues, reds, yellows and oranges.

On the reef slope, tall green coral trees grow upright in the spaces between coral heads and rock pinnacles, forming havens for clusters of fairy basslets and butterflyfishes. Look for big Napoleon wrasses cruising between the pinnacles, and remember, whale sharks are sometimes spotted here. The shallower north side of the channel – where submerged sand banks form hills and valleys are overgrown with thickets of coral – is home to dense concentrations of fishes. Groupers, colourful wrasses, occasional sea turtles and sting rays are all frequent visitors here. Photo opportunities abound.

Vadu Caves: This site runs along the outer north side of the atoll in the channel that separates North and South Malé atolls. Beginning at about 22m (72ft) are a series of caverns and overhangs running along

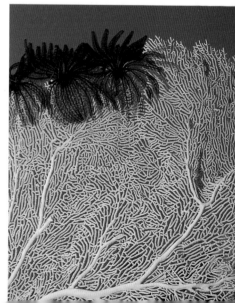

Sea fan with feather stars

the reef. They range in size from small to large. At 35m (115ft) are the larger caverns. Most of the caverns do not cut very deeply into the reef, but it is a good idea to bring along an underwater light for spotting smaller crustaceans like shrimps and crabs that inhabit the low light areas near the back walls. Look for small dragonets displaying their colourful dorsal fins in sandy areas near the walls of the caverns, and for clusters of small yellow sea fans that begin at 26m (85ft). Look out from the caverns occasionally to see the pelagic fishes go by. This is a nice spot for macro photography.

The outer reef near **Cocoa Island** and the pass just north of **Mafushi Island** are well known for the beautiful soft corals that grow there. A school of orange-tailed butterflyfish is often seen near the reef. Between **Ben Haa Falhu Reef** and **Gulhi Island** are some small pinnacles with lots of small fishes and lush coral growth.

Ari Atoll

Mushimasmagili (Fish Head Reef): A well known dive spot in Ari Atoll, this is a circular reef, centrally located in the eastern half of the atoll and is famous for its fine array of pelagic fishes, especially gray reef sharks. Schooling barracuda, tuna and jacks are often found in the clear waters here. Look for other sharks, turtles and manta rays often seen just off the reef.

Mayaafushi Thila: A submerged reef in the northern half of Ari Atoll. Lots of big fishes, like schooling barracuda, tuna, jacks and dozens of small white-tip reef sharks. Look around for black coral trees too. Near Halaveli is **Sting Ray City**, where you can feed sting rays as they flutter by.

Fesdu Wreck: A small boat that was sunk intentionally nine years ago, it sits at 27m (90ft)

A white-tip reef shark

and is covered with soft corals, attracts lots of fishes and makes an interesting dive. Farther north, near **Rasdu Atoll**, a school of hammerhead sharks is occasionally spotted. Kuramathi and Veligandu islands are the places to stay if you really want to see the hammerheads. Some resorts in north Ari Atoll organize diving excursions to this area.

Farther south in Ari Atoll are numerous dive sites, including the superb pass between **Dhagethi** and **Digurah** islands on the southeast side of the atoll. It includes three submerged reefs near Digurah island that are known for an abundance of pelagic fishes and rays. The north side of this pass has numerous beautifully coloured anemones and clownfish. Reefs along the outer southwest side of the atoll are said to support a lot of sharks, and the lagoon diving throughout this atoll is terrific.

A clownfish resting among anemone

Whales and manta rays are well-known in the southern part of Ari Atoll. **Manta Point**, on the outer southwest reef, is a good place to spot mantas between January and May. There is another Manta Point northwest of Ari Atoll.

Addu Atoll

Just south of the equator is **Addu**, the southernmost atoll in Maldives. It is a small atoll and like the others, surrounded by steep outer walls of coral and strong currents. A causeway built to link several of the islands in this atoll has cut down on the flow of water through it, and the lagoon diving is not up to the standards of those of the atolls to the north. There is a shipwreck in the lagoon near **Abuhera** island, but diving is not recommended here because the wreck still oozes oil in several places. However, along the outer walls of the atoll the visibility is excellent, and the profusion of corals and fishes truly amazing.

There is good diving in **Man Kandu** and **Gan** channels as well. Take note – strong currents and the remote location make this a diving destination for only the experienced diver. The remote location of this atoll accounts for the few divers that visit here, but for those that do, a pristine diving experience awaits them. There is only one resort here, the **Ocean Reef Club**. You can book your reservation through Phoenix Travels Pvt Ltd in Malé (Tel: 32-3181, Fax: 32-5499). There are weekly flights from Malé to Gan on Air Maldives; the plane is small and so is the luggage allowance.

– *Denise Tackett*

Few divers ever explore the waters of remote Addu Atoll

Activities

1. Watersports

Brilliant sunshine, optimum water temperature and excellent visibility make Maldives the ideal destination for a whole range of watersports like windsurfing, waterskiing, catamaran sailing, fishing and snorkelling. The shallow, calm waters that surround many islands provide the perfect learning grounds for novices starting off on their first lessons. The seas are calmest from November to April, but there are calm periods to be found from May to October when wind and rain are more likely.

Resorts normally charge an hourly, daily or weekly rate for the use of their sports facilities. Some, like Club Med, offer free use of windsurfing boards, catamarans, canoes and other equipment in their resort package. Beginner and advanced courses are generally conducted in English; other languages like German, Italian and French are also available, depending on the instructors available at the resort. For a higher fee, private tuition can be arranged. Most resorts offer almost the same variety of watersports although you should know that not all offer waterskiing and parasailing. If these are deciding factors in choosing a resort make sure you check with your travel agent when booking your package.

Windsurfing: Serious windsurfing buffs may find Maldives a little disappointing. The winds are moderate for most of the year, except in July and August when strong winds of over 20 knots will send your adrenaline racing. Unfortunately, this is also smack in the middle of the rainy season. Without a surf, it is plain slalom, speed sailing and cruising. Experienced windsurfers should choose resorts with large lagoons like Laguna and Thulaagiri, or else venture beyond the house reefs into open waters. The moderate winds during the dry season and calm lagoons, however, are perfect conditions for beginners and novices of the sport.

One of the hazards of windsurfing is the presence of coral heads in the shallow water. A good windsurfing instructor will point out these spots to you; if not, ask. For added protection, you should wear booties to protect yourself against coral cuts. On average a basic course will set you back US$150, with private lessons at US$35 an hour.

Catamaran sailing: Cutting through the waves with the wind in your face can be an exhilarating experience. Note that at some resorts, for safety reasons, staff will not rent out catamarans unless you produce a certificate proving your ability. Alternatively, hitch a ride with someone who is qualified. Rentals by the hour average US$30, and US$120 for the whole day. A basic course will cost you US$200 while private lessons are US$40 an hour.

Waterskiing: Many, but not all, resorts offer waterskiing. A good number of resorts do not allow waterskiing because of environmental reasons. Some say it scares the fish away. If you want to ski, verify availability before booking your package. The cost for 15 minutes of waterskiing is about US$30.

Parasailing: Few resorts offer this sport because of the risks involved and skilled staff required. For the uninitiated, parasailing involves wearing a body harness with an attached parachute and being lifted up over water while tethered to a moving speedboat. After being carried aloft for about 15 minutes, the boat comes to a gradual stop, you lose height and gently land on the beach. Parasailing

is a lot safer than it sounds, although some would hesitate at calling it a sport as no skill is required of the participant. The only pre-requisite is that you don't suffer from vertigo!

Only the following resorts offer parasailing: Rihiveli, Bandos, Angaga, Biyadoo, Kanifinolhu, Maayafushi and Villivaru. Average cost: US$35 per ride.

Surfing: This is an undiscovered surfer's paradise. Maldives has

classic reef breaks and lots of tube riding when the wind is right. Surfing season is from April through November. Apart from your own board, you need two things to surf here: a boat and someone who knows where the good waves are. For experienced surfers, Tony Hinde has both.

Hinde, who has been surfing in Maldives for 20 years, runs surfing safaris on his 20-m (65-ft) yacht-*dhoni Celeste*. He often visits the outer atolls in search of the perfect wave and usually finds it. The *Celeste* takes six to eight passengers with dormitory-style bunks and two private cabins. Fresh water showers and meals are provided. Cost: US$106 per person per day.

For those who prefer to be land-based, Hinde combines a stay at a resort in North Malé Atoll with all-day surfing adventures from his boat. Full-board price with lunch on the boat is US$65 to US$125 per person per day, depending on the quality of accommodation. For bookings contact: Foster Travel Services in Australia, Tel: 056-822155, Fax: 056-822965.

Dhoni sailing: Sail-*dhonis* are small, traditional wooden boats with triangular sails. They usually take a maximum of six people. Sailing trips take guests around the nearby waters. On a windy day, this can be a relaxing and enjoyable way to pass an afternoon. A minimum of two people is required. Cost: about US$10 an hour.

2. Snorkelling

With an abundance of healthy reefs that come within a few metres of the surface, Maldives is a snorkeller's delight. Good reefs are easily accessible from the beach at your resort. *Dhonis* also ferry guests to nearby reefs, often as part of an island-hopping excursion, or combined with a picnic.

Snorkelling is easy as no cumbersome gear or specialized training is needed: all you need is a mask, fins and snorkel, and lots of sunblock on your back. Gazing into the warm, clear water, you will see

A snap-happy snorkeller

hard corals in shades of pink, blue and lavender. Some corals look like masses of antlers tossed on the sand, others like flat, round tables or bouquets of pink-tipped flowers.

The brilliant colours of the corals are visible to the naked eye only by snorkelling in shallow water. Sea water absorbs colour as light passes through it, so the deeper you go, the less colour you see. The first to go is red, which starts to fall off at 3m (10ft), followed by orange and yellow. Although your eyes will compensate for this loss, the colours you see will always be diminished unless you restore them with a camera strobe or an underwater light.

In sandy areas, look for groups of black-and-white striped damselfish that hover above small corals, and for multi-coloured wrasses poking around in the sand for a meal of small crustaceans. Because these fishes have no fear of people, snorkelling in Maldives is like swimming through an aquarium.

If you see a lot of massive corals, look for parrotfish that munch these corals with their beak-like teeth in order to get at the algae they contain. Try to spot giant clams in the sand and smaller ones embedded in the massive corals.

Swim out to the end of the reef and have a look over the edge. You may see an orange cloud of fairy basslets near the reef, groups of gold-lined glowfish and all the way down, in the deep blue, giant pink sea fans that decorate the deeper reefs. Here, larger fishes like sweetlips, jacks and snappers, and schools of fusiliers glide past.

Snorkelling gear is available from the dive shop at your resort for US$5 to US$8 a day. If you have never snorkelled before, or if you have any questions about how to use a snorkel, someone at the dive shop will explain the technique to you. If you want to capture these beautiful reefs on film, Kodak and Fuji have disposable underwater cameras made just for snorkellers. The Fuji Quick Snap Marine and the Kodak Fun Aquatic are good down to 3m (10ft). They come already loaded with 24-exposure, ISO 400 film and are available at resorts for about US$20 each. The film can be processed and returned to you within a few hours, or a few days, depending on your location.

Snorkelling is fun and a great way to pass a few hours. But a note of caution – the combination of tropical sun and sea can give you a bad sunburn before you realize it. You should always use a waterproof sun block with a high SPF, especially on the back of your legs and shoulders, and wear a T-shirt for additional protection.

Never bring up any of the pretty corals, shells, or any other marine life you see. When taken out of their environment, these animals soon die and lose all their colour, and they start to smell.

3. Fishing

Although fishing is the economic lifeline of the Maldivians, fishing for big game fish as a sport is relatively unknown here, as compared to other Indian Ocean islands like Mauritius and Seychelles. There is, as yet, no organization in Maldives that promotes sportfishing, although this obviously has great potential with the teeming waters all around. Most resorts offer a range of day and night *dhoni* fishing activities for guests.

You can fish all year in Maldives, but rough sea conditions from June to September can cause cancellations at the last minute. On the eastern side of the atolls choppy seas can be a problem in December and January. *Dhoni* fishing expeditions can be half-day – lasting three to four hours in the morning – or full-day excursions. Night fishing is quite popular among resort guests as there is little to do in the evenings. Even in the unlikely event that you do not catch anything, the prospect of a night out at sea is a thrill by itself. Night fishing times can vary but the length of the trip is usually three hours or less. The expeditions are usually followed by barbecues on the beach, or else, the fish is prepared back at the resort for dinner.

Daytime trips generally go offshore to deeper waters where the catch is bonito, barracuda, yellowfin tuna and the like. Linefishing and trawling are the standard fishing techniques. At night you can expect to fish closer to the reef where linefishing is the norm. The catch is usually grouper and other reef fish. On average, a half-day trip by *dhoni* will cost US$30 and a night trip US$20 per person for a minimum number of four to 10 participants.

Some resorts offer deep-sea fishing from a speedboat; others, like Giraavaru use a modified yacht-*dhoni* for offshore fishing trips. These boats take four to six people and go offshore in search of big barracuda, sailfish and occasionally, marlin. The cost for a full day or night of deep-sea fishing ranges from US$320–US$500. Giraavaru's *Pegasus* is available for extended charter through Phoenix Hotels & Resorts Pvt Ltd. Vabbinfaru, Rihiveli and Kanifinolhu resorts also operate regular deep-sea fishing trips for their guests.

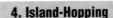

4. Island-Hopping

If you feel restless after a while and want to experience a bit of local colour, an island-hopping trip may be just the thing to do. Resorts normally offer a half-day trip by *dhoni* to a nearby fishing village, followed by a visit to another resort for a spot of snorkelling or a picnic.

Fishing villages, classified as 'inhabited islands', are strictly out of bounds to visi-

Hauling in a hefty catch

tors by government decree. You need a special permit from the Ministry of Atolls Administration to visit an inhabited island other than a resort. However, certain fishing villages are officially opened to tourists, and resort-organized excursions costing US$30 to US$45 per person are the closest you will ever get to sampling the local life.

The drawback of such a resort-organized excursion is that you cannot choose the village you wish to visit. This is decided by the resort operator, depending on the distance and travelling time from the resort you are staying at. As fishing villages are generally similar in character, the description of Dhagethi village on the facing page will give you an idea of what to expect.

Several inhabited islands open to visitors are found in North and South Malé and Ari atolls where most resorts are located. Resorts in North Malé Atoll may organize visits to the popular fishing villages at **Himmafushi** and **Hura** islands. If you are staying at one of the resorts in South Malé Atoll, one of the most visited islands nearby is Gulhi, once famous for its boat-builders but who are now markedly absent. Other popular destinations include **Guraidhu** and **Diffhushi** islands.

For those staying in Ari Atoll, there are many lovely fishing villages to discover, among them **Thoddu** where the ruins of an ancient Buddhist temple have been found. Thoddu is also famous for its watermelons, which the locals relish during the fasting months. **Rasdhu**, **Feridhu**, **Dhagethi** and **Dhigurah** are other islands frequented by resort excursions in this atoll.

While urbanization is fast catching up in Malé, the other inhabited islands have remained largely unchanged in many ways. Over the years, many of these fishing villages, like Himmafushi and Hura, have been affected by tourism, evidenced by the long row of small tourist shops that greet the visitor at the islands. Nevertheless, they still offer an interesting insight into traditional Maldivian lifestyle.

Village life at Hura in North Malé Atoll

A Visit to Dhagethi

Twenty minutes by *dhoni* from Kuda Rah, we arrive at the island of Dhagethi – home to some 500 people – on the southeast rim of Ari Atoll. From a distance, an old *nika* tree rises tall above the top of the palm trees. My guide Ismail explains that this tree is of particular importance, serving as a navigational guide for boats especially at night. The water around Dhagethi is surprisingly clear

Plucking curry leaves

and the white sandy beach clean. From the jetty, you can see right across the island to the sea at the other end.

A flurry of excited children run up to the jetty to greet us: Ismail is obviously popular with the people here. A couple of tourist shops selling souvenirs line the road leading up from the beach. Among them is a provision shop, a cramped little store that provides basic household essentials for the village folk. As in all fishing villages, a main coral-paved road

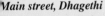

Main street, Dhagethi

runs through the island. From this, side-roads branch out leading to a maze of narrow paths and houses.

The simple houses are made of coral and wood with thatched roofs of native *cadjan*, dried palm leaves threaded together with coir rope. Outside the houses are a couple of *jorli*, hammock-like chairs in which one can relax and chat with passing neighbours, or while away the afternoon. A coral wall surrounding the compound provides a measure of privacy, enclosing a garden and an open-air bathroom.

The interiors of the houses are simply furnished. Perhaps the most comfortable place for a siesta is the *undhoali* outside, a wooden bed strung up by coir rope under the shade of a big tree.

On one end of the beach, a group of

Swinging on an undhoali

women dry out salted fish on wooden racks under the blazing sun. While the men go out fishing, the women tend to their homes and children: in some villages, women are involved in handicraft activities like coir-making and mat-weaving.

In many fishing villages, especially those around Malé, you will notice a scarcity of men. Many have abandoned fishing and taken up jobs in the capital or the resorts, leaving their families behind. Some only return after a year to spend a month with their families before returning to their jobs.

Fortunately, there is a strong communal feeling among the villagers and close ties between families. The menfolk's prolonged absences also explains the many half-built houses you see throughout the village. I am told that the average Maldivian takes about three years to build his house, simply because he is never around to complete it.

In an open area, a big wooden shed serves as the village kindergarten where lessons are conducted with blackboard and chalk in native *Divehi*. Here, where television and computer games have yet to invade, children content themselves with playing games on the beach and swimming in the lagoons. By age 10 though, most boys would have mastered two very important basic skills: sailing and fishing.

On the beach on the other side of the island is the boat-making area. Similar in form to the Arabian *dhow*, the hull of the *dhoni* is made of coconut trunks and reinforced with imported timber. Without a blueprint, the art of *dhoni*-making has been passed down through practice and word of mouth.

It takes a team of four to five carpenters, called

The traditional craft of dhoni making

kissaru vadin, about 40 days to build a standard 10m-long (33ft) *dhoni*. When completed, fish oil is smoothed over the hull of the fishing *dhoni* to ensure a smooth and safe journey and protect it from wood rot. Practically every family owns a *dhoni* of some size. Despite mechanization, the basic form of the *dhoni* has seen few changes; many still maintain their triangular cotton sails.

Back in the village, Ismail's friends have specially prepared a Maldivian tea for us of *gula* (fish balls), *telali bambukeo* (fried breadfruit), *keku* (fluffy cake) and *kiri sa* (tea with milk and sugar). As we eat, members of the family sit around, laughing and chatting.

A noon-day meal

In one corner, an old lady smokes the *guru-guda* or hubble-bubble (so named from the sound produced by the bubbles in the glass container). She inhales deeply from the mixture of imported tobacco and syrup drawn from the sap of the coconut tree.

It promises an exhilarating feeling I am told. I take a deep drag of the smoke that envelopes the woman, and on that high note we take our leave.

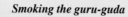

Smoking the guru-guda

5. Hummingbird Excursions

Besides providing airport transfers, Hummingbird Helicopter Services offers a variety of excursions that enable you to combine trips to remote islands and take in spectacular aerial views of Maldives. 'Flips' are 15-minute long helicopter tours of the islands surrounding Malé or your nearest helipad. There is no better way to see the expanse of the blue rings of the atolls and the many islands that make up Maldives. Make sure you bring your camera along as photo opportunities are fantastic. Cost: US$59.

Hummingbird also organizes several full-day picnics to uninhabited islands. The Robinson Crusoe Picnic leaves at 9am and takes

you on a 30-minute flight from the airport to **Kandolodhu** in Ari Atoll – an uninhabited island with a lovely stretch of beach – where a welcome drink awaits you. There is a fishing trip to the nearby reefs or you can snorkel on the house reef. Remember to bring your snorkelling gear along. A barbecue lunch is served, with grilled fish, salads and a generous selection of fresh fruits, followed by more snorkelling or plain lazing around until departure at about 5pm. Cost: US$149 per person.

The Sunrise Island Picnic combines an aerial flight with a visit to a fishing village. The excursion takes guests on a spectacular 15-minute flight at 9.30am before landing on the fishing village of **Guraidhu** in South Malé Atoll. Follow-

barbecue lunch awaits

ing a tour of the village, you travel by boat to Rihiveli. From here it is a walk or wade, depending on the tide, across to the uninhabited **Sunrise Island** where a barbecue lunch is served. At about 3.30pm, it's back to Guraidhu for an opportunity to pick up a few souvenirs from the village's tourist shops before flying back to the airport. Cost: US$99 per person.

Bookings for the aerial tours and picnics can be made at the resorts, or you can contact Hummingbird directly for more details. The Mi-8 helicopter takes a maximum of 20 passengers on each flight. Transfers from the resort to the airport or helipad are not included. Hummingbird Helicopter Services can be contacted at MHA Building, 4th Floor, No 1 Orchid Magu, Malé. Tel: 32-5708, Fax: 32-3161.

6. Cruising

Cruising safaris are gaining much popularity these days as an alternative to staying on an island resort. There are a number of tour operators in Malé which organize boat cruises for a minimum number of people. Prices vary with the kind of boat used and the number of persons in the group. At the high end are luxury yachts with air-conditioning, individual showers and posh fittings. If your budget is limited, consider a converted *dhoni* with more basic facilities. Yacht-*dhonis* – a cross between a cargo boat and a cabin cruiser – are the most popular among cruise-operators. Most cruise operators will include diving as well for an extra fee. For information on diving safaris, see *Diving*.

Voyages Maldives (Tel: 32-3019, Fax: 32-5336), one of the most established tour operators in Maldives, offers a variety of packages for cruising. An eight-day trip begins from the airport or Malé, cruising to uninhabited islands, fishing villages and resort islands in the North and South Malé atolls. The course is tailored to suit individual groups. Voyages Maldives has nine yacht-*dhonies* for hire. The costs depends on the number of persons and the boat used. The *Blue* (20m/65½ft), *Gulfaam* (20m/65½ft), *Sea Coral* (19m/62ft) and *Sea Farer* (18m/59ft) come with private cabins, toilets, freshwater showers and cater for 10 to 14 passengers. The cost of full-board accommodation is about US$70 per person a day.

Phoenix Hotels and Resorts Pvt Ltd (Tel: 32-3181, Fax: 32-5499) has several safari boats that cruise North and South Malé, Ari, Baa, Felidu and Lhaviyani atolls. The yacht-*dhonis* cost US$70 per person per day, full board and take 8–12 passengers.

The Munaa, a beautiful double-masted sailing ship, runs seven-day cruises in North and South Malé atolls. *The Munaa* is 24-m (78½-ft) long and takes six to 12 passengers in six cabins. The full-board cost is US$55 per person per day. The booking agent in Europe is TUI. In Maldives contact Meeru Island Resort, Tel: 44-3157.

The Munaa

Practical Information

GETTING THERE

most all visitors arrive in Maldives by
, landing at Malé International Air-
rt on the island of Hulhule. About 70
ternational and chartered flights land
ch week. From Europe, the main air-
es are Balair, LTU, Condor, Lauda, Air
00 and Alitalia. ZAS and Emirates air-
es fly from the Middle East. Asian air-
es with flights to Maldives are Air In-
a, Air Pakistan, Eva Airlines, Air Lanka
d Singapore Airlines. Most flights from
rope arrive in the day, providing visi-
rs with an excellent aerial introduction
Maldives. There are no direct air ser-
es from Australia or North America
d travellers have to fly to Europe or
ia first.

TRAVEL ESSENTIALS

hen to Visit

nerally, the best time to visit Maldives
during the dry northeast monsoon from
te November to April. This period is
arked by lots of sunshine, blue skies
d little rainfall. The sea also tends to
calm and water visibility is at its best.
is is the high season and resorts are of-
n fully booked at this time. The low
ason is from May to October during the
uthwest monsoon. This is the wet sea-
n and the weather is less predictable,
th heavy rainfall sometimes accompa-
ed by very strong winds. The sea can
t pretty rough. Although the two peri-
s are quite distinct, there may be weeks

Malé International Airport

of sunshine in July and August and showers in February and March.

Passports and Visas

Make sure that your international passport is valid for at least six months. A
30-day visa is issued upon arrival at the
airport. Nationals from Bangladesh, India, Pakistan and Italy are issued 90-day
visas on arrival. Israeli passport holders
are barred from entry. A two-month visa
extension can be obtained from the Department of Immigration in Malé for
Rf300.

Health and Vaccinations

Yellow fever vaccinations are required for
visitors coming from affected areas.
Malaria is not a problem in Maldives but
mosquitoes can be a nuisance. A good
mosquito repellent is advisable. There is
generally little problem with food but

some visitors may suffer from diarrhoea and upset stomach because of the change in diet. Avoid drinking unboiled water. Drinking water is supplied at the resorts and bottles of mineral water are readily available. Sun-worshippers should guard against over-exposure, especially those coming from temperate climates. Allow your body time to acclimatize. Always use a sun block with a high SPF and drink lots of water to prevent dehydration.

Customs

Customs check at Malé International Airport is a thorough affair. This is a Muslim country and local sensitivities have to be observed. No alcohol, pork products,

Airport jetty

pornographic material or idols of worship are to be brought in. Firearms, ammunition and drugs are also prohibited. Visitors are allowed to bring in tobacco for personal consumption. The export of tortoiseshell and corals, except in ornamental form, is illegal and heavy penalties are imposed on traffickers.

Weather

Maldives has a tropical climate, with an average daily temperature of 25°–32°C throughout the year. At night, the temperature drops by about three degrees. Water temperature is 28°–30°C all year through and is ideal for most watersports. Humidity is high, about 75 to 80 percent, though this is tolerable with the cool ocean breezes.

Clothing

Lightweight cotton clothes are best. During the rainy season, a light raincoat may come in handy. While resort dressing is informal, visitors to

A tropical paradise

Malé and fishing villages should dr with some decorum. Women should co their thighs, avoid see-through cloth and bikini-tops. T-shirts and shorts a quite acceptable for men, but no bar of the torso please. For visits to t mosques, a sarong is required. Sunbathi in the nude is not allowed at resorts.

Electricity

Most resorts have generators that provi power 24 hours a day. Electricity is 2 volts AC50Hz. The standard round p European plug is increasingly replaced square pin models.

Time Differences

The Maldives is five hours ahead of GM Some resorts set their clocks ahead to low guests to enjoy a longer day. T practice also allows ample time for a port transfers, especially for resorts fu ther from the airport.

Geography

Maldives is part of the Laccadives-Chag ridge that runs north and south for ov 2,000km (1,243 miles) in the eastern I dian Ocean. Located south of India a 670km (416 miles) west of Sri Lank Maldives is a double strand of atoll straddling the equator and stretchi over 800km (495 miles) long and 130k (81 miles) wide. For an explanation atoll formation, see *Diving*. The land ar of Maldives is less than one percent of i territory and consists of 1,190 small i lands, most of which are less than 2 (6ft) above sea level. There are many mo sand bars and coral outcrops to be foun Approximately 200 islands are inhabite and at present, another 70 are leased o as resorts. The rest are uninhabited.

Malé, the capital island, is centrally located and is the focal point for all administrative and governmental affairs in Maldives. The atolls have been regrouped into 19 administrative atolls, often with a change in name.

Air Maldives provides regular service to some of the outlying islands, but inter-island transport is usually limited to travel by *dhoni* or inter-atoll ferry. Sailing from Malé to the southernmost atoll can take two days or more, depending on sea and weather conditions.

Government and Economy

The government is divided into three levels – that of island, atoll and nation. Each inhabited island is ruled by a *kateeb* or island chief who is responsible for minor judicial matters and the general management of his island, including nearby uninhabited islands. The *kateeb* reports to the *atolu verin* or atoll chief by walkie-talkie each day. The atoll chief is in charge of the economic and political welfare of the atoll. He is assisted by a group of *gazis* who attend to judicial matters. Overseeing all the atolls is the nation's central government in Malé, over which the President has supreme power. Every five years the President is first nominated by the Citizens' Majlis, comprising two representatives from each atoll, two from Malé and eight Presidential nominees. The President is then elected by national referendum.

In a country vastly lacking in land resources, Maldives is fortunately blessed with rich waters and beautiful islands that account for the country's two main industries – fishing and tourism. By far, fishing is the main occupation, employing 22 percent of the working population. Fish exports form more than 70 percent of the total exports.

Tourism is the most dynamic sector of the economy and the highest foreign revenue earner. Since the establishment of the first resort in 1972, 70 resorts islands have been developed. In 1992, tourist arrivals were almost 236,000. Resorts have been largely concentrated in North and South Malé and Ari atolls, and plans are underway to expand the tourist belt.

A local lass

Population

Maldivians are a mixed race, a result of contact with the many seafaring civilizations of the past. Most notable are the Indian, Sri Lankan and Arabic influences. The population is about 220,000, of which about 25 percent live in Malé.

Religion

Islam is the national religion. The people are Sunni Muslims of the Shafi'ite sect, one of the most liberal of Islamic sects. Religion is the backbone of the society and a strong governing force. The tenets of Islam form the basis of the judiciary system.

Language

Divehi, the national language, is derived from the Indo-Iranian language group and is related to ancient Sinhala from Sri Lanka. It contains many words of Tamil and Arabic origin. The written form of *Divehi* is called *Thaana* and was introduced in mid-15th century. It is written from right to left and contains 24 letters, nine of which are derived from Arabic numerals. Accent marks above and below the letters indicate vowel sounds.

English is widely spoken in Malé and at resorts. You will hear a smattering of European languages and Japanese in tourist-frequented areas.

MONEY MATTERS

Currency

The local currency is the Maldivian *rufiyaa* (Rf). Each *rufiyaa* is divided into 100 *larees*. Notes come in denominations of Rf 500, 100, 50, 20, 10, 5 and 2. Coins are in Rf1, and 50, 25, 10, 5, 2 and 1 *laree*. At press time, one US$1 was equivalent to about Rf11. The US dollar is widely accepted in Maldives. Foreign currency can be exchanged for *rufiyaa* through authorized money-changers in Malé, banks and resorts. Some shops in Malé will change US dollars for customers, but usually at a lower rate. There is no black market and no restrictions on the amount when changing cash or travellers' cheques. Change only what is necessary. The *rufiyaa* is not accepted outside Maldives. At most resorts, bills are charged to the room account and payable by credit card or travellers' cheques, so there is little need for local currency.

Credit Cards

Major credit cards are acceptable at resorts, and in major shops and restaurants in Malé.

VISA/MASTERCARD/JCB
(c/o Cyprea Travels)
25 Marine Drive, Malé
Tel: 32-2451; Fax: 32-2523

AMERICAN EXPRESS
(c/o Universal Travels)
18 Marine Drive, Malé
Tel: 32-3116; Fax: 32-2695

Tipping

Tipping is not a rule, but as in everywhere else, widely appreciated. There is no standard rate but US$1 is a fair amount for good service rendered.

Taxes

There is a daily bed tax of US$6 which is included in the price of your accommodations. For visitors leaving Maldives, there is an airport tax of US$10.

GETTING AROUND

Airport Transfers

Most tourists arriving in Maldives come on pre-arranged packages which include transfers from the airport to resorts. Transfers are usually by *dhonis*, though some resorts may use speedboats. Depending on the location of the resorts, the ride can take from 15 minutes to three hours. For those staying at Ari Atoll resorts, transfers are made by speedboat or helicopter. Hummingbird Heli-

copter Services has nine helipads strate, cally located throughout the central ato from which *dhoni* rides to resorts are l than 30 minutes. Note that helicop transfers are only provided during t day. Should you arrive at night, you w have to spend a night in Malé and w for your transfer the next day. One-w transfers to resorts cost between US$ and US$179, depending on the distanc

Verify the transfer arrangements a fees with your travel agent when boc ing. Confusion can sometimes arise at t airport, especially at peak hours. If y should be left stranded, approach the i formation desk at the airport for ass tance. If you are on your own, hop or *dhoni* to Malé and check out the tour c erators there.

A traditional dho

Dhoni

Inter-island transport is usually by *dho* Resorts have their own *dhonis* and spee boats which provide for airport transfe excursions and other needs. The bigg resorts have a fleet of boats for hir Costs can be high: as much as US$60 . hour plus fuel. Tour agencies in Ma also have boats for hire. From Malé, ta *dhonis* are available for hire along t waterfront. These ply back and for from the airport to Malé for about US per passenger. From Malé to the resor the charges vary with the distance a the number of persons travelling. Che with resort agents for prices and sche

ed departures, or if you have time and
tience, check with individual boat own-
s along the waterfront. You can expect
pay US$15 for a *dhoni* to Kurumba,
5 minutes from Malé. The price is for
e entire boat, not per person.

ir

ir Maldives operates regularly scheduled
ights to distant atolls like Addu and
aamu. It is not likely that the average
ourist would be flying to any of these is-
nds, unless it is to the Ocean Reef Club
n the island of Gan in Addu Atoll.
ransfers between Malé and most resorts
n be arranged with Hummingbird Heli-
pter Services.

HOURS AND HOLIDAYS

usiness Hours

ffice hours are Saturday–Thursday
30am–1.30pm. Shop hours are Satur-
ay–Thursday 8am–11pm, Friday
pm–11pm. Banks are open Sunday–
hursday 9am–1pm, Saturday 9am–
1am. Most offices and shops close for a
w minutes each day for prayers. Prayer
mes are around 5.30am, noon, 3pm,
pm and 7pm. During *Ramadan*, the fast-
g month, office hours are shortened to
am–1pm. Shops open later, about 11am
nd close from 6pm–8pm for dinner.

ublic Holidays

ost of the holidays are Islamic ones
ased on the lunar calendar. The most
gnificant event of the year is the fasting
onth of *Ramadan* which falls 11 days
rlier each year. The sighting of the new
oon marks the end of the fasting month
nd *Kuda Id* follows with a big celebra-
on marked by much feasting and rejoic-
g. Two months and 10 days later is the
elebration of *Bodu Id* when those who
an afford it depart for the *haj*, the holy
ilgrimage to Mecca. The Islamic New

Year and the Prophet Mohammed's birth-
day are celebrated as holidays.

The non-Islamic holidays which fall on
fixed dates are:

New Year's Day	1 January
Independence Day	26 July
Victory Day	3 November
Republic Day	11 November

ACCOMMODATION

Apart from accommodation featured under the *Resorts* section, the ones listed here
merit consideration. Price ranges indicated here are for a standard double room
(with full board, unless otherwise stated)
for one night during the high season:

$	=	under US$150
$$	=	US$151–US$200
$$$	=	US$201–US$250
$$$$	=	above US$250

North Malé Atoll

HELENGELI
Manta Reisen
Marine Drive, Malé
Tel: 32-5587, Fax: 32-5625
About 44km (27¼ miles) or almost four
hours by *dhoni* from the airport, this
pleasant resort has accommodation in
coral stone bungalows with thatched
roofs. It has an excellent house reef (over
2km/1¼ mile long) and the remote location means you almost never run into another dive boat. The clientele is mostly
Swiss. *$*

THULAAGIRI
H Jazeera
Marine Drive 15, Malé
Tel: 32-5529, Fax: 32-1026
Twenty minutes (10km/6¼ miles) from
the airport by speedboat, Thulaagiri was

Thulaagiri

the first Club Med resort in Maldives but is now locally-owned. The resort has 59 Maldivian-style thatched-roof bungalows with air-conditioning and hot and cold desalinated water. There are fresh-water swimming pools along the beach. Well-known for its fine food, this resort serves breakfast, lunch and dinner buffets prepared by a European chef. Popular with Europeans and Japanese. *$$*

GIRAAVARU
Phoenix Hotels & Resorts
Marine Drive, Malé
Tel: 32-3181, Fax: 32-5499
Only 12km (7½ miles) from the airport, this resort has 48 air-conditioned rooms with hot and cold desalinated water. All rooms have baths, hair dryers and IDD telephones. There is a fresh-water swimming pool in addition to the standard water sports, and Giraavaru offers deep sea fishing expeditions. The clientele is largely Italian and German. *$$*

BAROS HOLIDAY RESORT
Universal Enterprises
38 Orchid Magu, Malé
Tel: 32-3971, Fax: 32-2676
Baros is located 16km (10 miles) north-west of the airport. The resort has 56 rooms with hot and cold desalinated water and 19 water bungalows. Some rooms have air-conditioning, others are fan-cooled. A range of water sports is available and the diving school is run by VIT. Food outlets include a coffee-shop and barbecue and buffet restaurants. Popular with the British and Germans.
$ (breakfast only)

FULL MOON RESORT (FURANA)
Universal Enterprises
38 Orchid Magu, Malé
Tel: 32-3080, Fax: 32-2678

Located 3km (2 miles) north of the airport, this 5-star resort has 156 air-conditioned rooms with hot and cold desalinated water. There are water bungalows built on stilts on the secluded north side of this large island. The full range of water sports is available. Restaurants include a pizza outlet, and Western, barbecue, Mediterranean and Thai restaurants. Attracts a cosmopolitan crowd.
$ (breakfast only)

NAKATCHAFUSHI TOURIST RESORT
Universal Enterprises
38 Orchid Magu, Malé
Tel: 32-2971, Fax: 32-2678
Twenty-four km (15 miles) from the airport, this resort has 51 air-conditioned bungalows with thatched roofs. All bungalows have baths with hot and cold desalinated water. The island has a large lagoon for sailing, windsurfing and waterskiing. The open-air restaurant serves buffet meals and there is an à la carte coffee-shop. The clientele is mainly British and German. *$*

BODUHITHI CORAL ISLE
Safari Tours
S E K No 1, Chandhani Magu, Malé
Tel: 32-3524, Fax: 32-2516
Located almost 30km (18½ miles) from the airport on the west side of the atoll, Boduhithi has 87 bungalows with and without air-conditioning and hot water. There are some water bungalows perched on the lagoon. Aerobics classes and most water sports are available. The clientele is largely German and French with some Japanese. *$$*

Full Moon Resort

outh Malé Atoll

VAADHU DIVING PARADISE
Maarandhooge Irumatheebai, Malé
Tel: 32-5844, Fax: 44-3397
Located 8km (5 miles) from the airport, on the south side of the channel separating North and South Malé atolls, this resort caters to Japanese divers and honeymooners. There is hot and cold desalinated water, air-conditioning and a choice of villas or water cottages/suites with private balconies. The luxurious water cottages feature a unique glass-top coffee table which lets you to enjoy the multicoloured fish swimming below. Vaadhu has an excellent house reef. *$$$$*

KANDOOMA TOURIST RESORT
46 Orchid Magu, Malé
Tel: 32-3360, Fax: 32-6880
Kandooma – 27km (17 miles) south of the airport and two hours by *dhoni* or 15 minutes by helicopter – is situated in the Guradu Channel. The individual bungalows have desalinated, but not hot water. The main restaurant serves continental food and there is a separate coffee-shop. The clientele is mainly German, Swiss and Dutch. *$*

OLHUVELI VIEW HOTEL
Ma Onyx
3/37 Chandhani Magu, Malé
Tel: 31-3645, Fax: 31-3646
Located 35km (22 miles) south of the airport, this resort caters to an affluent Italian and Japanese clientele. Exclusive water bungalows and suites with baths are available. All rooms have air-conditioning and hot and cold desalinated wa-

Vaadhu Diving Paradise

ter. Full board arrangements include buffet meals at the main restaurant. There are also à la carte Western and Japanese Teppanyaki restaurants. *$$$$*

PALM TREE ISLAND (VELIGANDHU HURA)
Crown Company Pte Ltd
Orchid Magu, Malé
Tel: 32-2432, Fax: 32-4009
About 30 minutes by speedboat from the airport, Palm Tree Island has 16 private bungalows with hot and cold desalinated water and individual terraces. The island is connected by what must be the longest jetty in Maldives to the neighbouring resort of Dhigufinolhu and the island of Bodu Huraa. The water around the three islands are ideal for snorkelling, with an impressively rich reef in shallow waters. The island is reputedly popular with honeymooners. *$$$*

Palm Tree Island bungalow

Ari Atoll

ELLAIDHOO TOURIST RESORT
Safari Tours, S E K No. 1
Chandhani Magu, Malé
Tel: 32-3524, Fax: 32-2516
Ellaidhoo, some 50km (31 miles) from the airport, is centrally located in eastern Ari Atoll. The resort caters to Austrian divers and is reputed to have the best house reef in all of Maldives. In order to let its guests enjoy the reef without getting wet, an underwater video camera has been installed on the reef. This feeds the video monitor in the bar and lets you watch the colourful marine life below. All bungalows are located along the beach to take advantage of fresh ocean breezes. No hot water here. *$*

MADOOGALI RESORT
Hermosa Ltd
H Gaadhoo, Malé
Tel: 32-3223, Fax: 32-7442
Madoogali is found in northwest Ari Atoll, about 72km (44½ miles) from the airport. All rooms are thatched roof bungalows with hot and cold desalinated water. Most water sports are available. The restaurant serves buffet meals with an emphasis on Italian dishes. The clientele is mainly Italian with some Austrian and German guests. *$$*

TWIN ISLAND (MAAFUSHIVARU)
Universal Enterprises
38 Orchid Magu, Malé
Tel: 32-3971, Fax: 32-2678
About 90km (56 miles) from the airport, this resort is located next to a helipad – its twin island. Nearby is the fishing village of Dhagethi and some of the best diving in the atoll. The resort has 32 air-conditioned bungalows with hot and cold desalinated water. Water bungalows are available too. The clientele is mainly Italian and German. *$$*

ARI BEACH RESORT (DIDDHU FINOLHU)
52 Marine Drive, Malé
Tel: 32-7354, Fax: 32-7355
Located some 104km (64½ miles) from the airport, this resort has its own helipad. There are 83 beach bungalows with patios, desalinated water and air-conditioning. There is a large lagoon for watersports (but no house reef) and a good windsurfing school. The main restaurant serves buffet meals and there is an à la carte coffee-shop. Attracts a cosmopolitan crowd. *$*

Felidu Atoll

ALIMATHA AQUATIC RESORT
Safari Tours
S E K No 1, Chandhani Magu, Malé
Tel: 32-3524, Fax: 32-2516
About 50km (31 miles) south of the airport, this is one of two resorts in Felidu Atoll. Alimatha is a Club Vacanze resort housing 70 air-conditioned bungalows with hot and cold fresh water. The usual water sports are offered and the diving is excellent. The clientele is Italian. Most

sporting activities are included in the f board room rate. *$*

Malé

In the unlikely event that you decide stay in Malé – resort guests may be forc to do this if boat transfers are not pos ble because of bad weather – you shou know that apart from two established h tels, facilities at the capital are relativ expensive and basic. The following a price categories for a double room, i cluding tax and breakfast:

$$ *$* = under US$50 $$
$$ *$$* = US$50–US$75 $$

Hotels

NASANDHURA PALACE HOTEL
Marine Drive
Tel: 32-3380, Fax: 32-0822
The Nasandhura Palace Hotel has a go location along Marine Drive, with a jet just in front. The hotel has a restaura and coffee-house with food at reasonab prices. Rooms are air-conditioned. *$$*

HOTEL ALIA
Haveeru Higun
Tel: 32-2080, Fax: 32-5499
Located on the west side of Malé, on road parallel to Marine Drive. Air-cond tioned rooms. *$$*

Guest Houses

There are many guest-houses located a over Malé which offer bed and breakfa at lower prices. Some have air-cond tioned rooms and private showers whi those at the lower end may have commo baths. Fresh water is not always readi available and rain water is sometim used instead. In some cases, a little pri negotiation may be worthwhile, esp cially if you are staying for more tha three days. Price categories are the sam as hotels.

ATHAMAA PALACE
Majeedhee Magu
Tel: 32-0370
This has some of the most appealing a commodation in Malé. This narrow bloc on the main street has pleasantly fur nished rooms, with hot and cold bath

nd shower. Each room has an attached
alcony where you can watch the street
ctivity below. The place is usually fully
ooked by visiting businessmen and gov-
rnment officials. *$$*

OOFARU TOURIST LODGE
O Box 21 Marine Drive
el: 32-2731
 cosy little guest-house on the east side
f Malé, near the Dragon Restaurant.
ou can watch locals enjoying the latest
raze of board-surfing just in front of
Joofaru. Rooms are air-conditioned and
esh water is available on request. *$*

RELAX INN
Jenveiru, Ameer Ahmed Magu
el: 31-4531/2, Fax: 31-4533
Located behind the Nasandhura Palace
Iotel, this 5-storey block houses 31 air-
onditioned rooms with hot water, TV
nd IDD phones. An elevator serves the
ifferent floors, a recently introduced
neans of mobility on this capital island.
here is a good restaurant and a day
oom service is available for less than five
ersons at US$35. This is especially use-
il for those who need a place to rest be-
ore a late night flight. *$$*

HEALTH AND EMERGENCIES

Medical Services

SWISS-AMDC CLINIC
Cathy Rose, Dharumavantha Magu,
O Box 20116, Malé
el: 32-5979, Fax: 32-5978

CENTRAL HOSPITAL

Most tourists are referred to the Swiss-
AMDC Clinic for medical needs. The clinic
is operated by two qualified Swiss doc-
tors, a professional laboratory technician
and a team of nurses.

Opening hours: Saturdays–Wednesdays
9.15am–12.30pm/6.15pm–8.45pm,
Thursdays 9.15am–12.30pm. Closed on
Fridays and public holidays.

Recompression Chambers

Recompression chambers are located at
Bandos, Club Med, Kuda Rah and Alimatha resorts. In case of emergencies, helicopter services can be arranged from remote resorts to the airport. Speedboat and
dhoni transport are also available. Your
resort will handle all arrangements. Travel
and diving insurance is recommended because medical costs are very high.

CENTRAL HOSPITAL
Sosun Magu, Malé
Tel: 32-4200
Offers basic medical services.

Pharmacies

There are a number of pharmacies in
Malé, especially along Majeedhee Magu,
which carry a wide range of basic medi-
cation and first-aid needs. Open
8.30am–11pm.

AMDC PHARMACY
(next to AMDC Clinic)
Dharumavantha Magu
Tel: 32-5979

ROOTS PHARMACY
(opposite Central Hospital)
Sosun Magu
Tel: 32-2083

CRESCENT PHARMACY
44 Majeedhee Magu
Tel: 32-0349

Crime

In general, Maldives is a safe place. The
crime rate is low, and the locals are generally courteous, but shy of foreigners.
Maldivians have an unusual form of punishment that has been criticized as being
too lenient. A person who commits a

crime is banished to a remote island away from his family for a period of time.

Police

The Maldivian police force is the National Security Service guards. You see them on the streets with their dark green uniforms.

COMMUNICATIONS AND NEWS

Postal Services

The post office in Malé is located along Chandhani Magu, with a bright red mail box in front. Airmail to Europe takes about a week. Open Saturday–Thursday 7.30am–12.30pm and 1.30pm–5.50pm. At resorts, the front-desk staff will handle ordinary mail for guests.

Courier services

All major courier services and EMS Speedpost are available in Malé. Resorts will make all the necessary arrangements for you.

Media

The two daily newspapers, the *Haveeru* and *Aafathi*, both carry a section in English. TV Maldives broadcasts mainly in *Divehi* with some English programming. The English news is on at 9pm for 30 minutes. At some resorts, there is a common TV room and CNN is available at certain times of the day. The Voice of Maldives radio has two stations, with the English news at 6pm.

Communications

The telecommunications station Dhiraagu is one of the most advanced in the region. Telex, fax and overseas telephone services are available at the station's office at the junction of Chandhani Magu and Fareedhee Magu. Telephone cards are available for Rf20 (for local calls), Rf200 and Rf500. Telephone card booths can be found outside the office. There are also coin booths for local calls.

Hours: Saturday–Thursday 7.30am–8pm; Friday and public holidays 8am–6pm.

IDD is available at some of the up-market resorts, otherwise make your call through the resort operator. US phone credit cards are not yet in use here.

USEFUL ADDRESSES

Key Government Offices

MINISTRY OF TOURISM
2nd Flr, Ghaazee Building
Ameer Ahmed Magu, Malé
Tel: 32-3224, Fax: 32-2512
Telex: 66019 TOURISM MF

DEPARTMENT OF IMMIGRATION
2nd Flr, Huravee Building
Ameer Ahmed Magu, Malé
Tel: 32-3913

MINISTRY OF ATOLLS ADMINISTRATION
Faashanaa Building
Marine Drive, Malé
Tel: 32-2826

MINISTRY OF INFORMATION
3rd Flr, Huvaree Building
Ameer Ahmed Magu, Malé
Tel: 32-3837

Travel Agencies

CYPREA HOTELS & TRAVELS PVT LTD
25 Marine Drive, Malé
Tel: 32-2451/32-5367, Fax: 32-3523
Telex: 66026 CYPTREA MF

PHOENIX TRAVELS PVT LTD
Fasmeeru
Marine Drive, Malé
Tel: 32-3181, Fax: 32-5499

AFARI TOURS
handhani Magu, Malé
el: 32-3524, Fax: 32-2516

NIVERSAL ENTERPRISES LTD
rchid Magu, Malé
el: 32-3080, Fax: 32-2678

OYAGES MALDIVES
areedhee Magu, Malé
el: 32-3019, Fax: 32-5336
elex: 66063 VOYAGESMF

irline Offices

ll airlines can be contacted through Air
Maldives Services, located behind MHA
uilding, Tel: 31-4808.

FURTHER READING

The Maldives Islands: Monography on the History, Archaeology and Epigraphy by H C P Bell. Colombo Printer, 1940.

Journey through Maldives by Mohamed Amin, Duncan Willetts and Peter Marshall. Camerapix Publishers International, Nairobi 1992.

Living Reefs of the Maldives by Dr R C Anderson. Novelty Printers and Publishers, Malé.

The Maldive Mystery by Thor Heyerdahl. George Allen & Unwin, London 1986.

The Maldives – a profile by Hassan Maniku. Department of Information, Malé 1977.

ACKNOWLEDGMENTS

Cover (T)	**Didier Noirot**
Cover (B), Back Cover	**Larry Tackett**
Photography	**Didier Noirot** *and*
Pages 5B, 13M, 13B, 14B, 17, 20B, 29B, 30B, 31, 33B, 34, 43B, 44T, 45T, 49, 56T, 59, 60T, 60B, 61T, 61B, 62T, 62B, 64, 65B, 66, 68T, 74B, 75, 76T, 79T, 79B, 80M, 80B, 81T, 81B, 82, 84B, 85, 86, 87T	**Larry Tackett**
43T, 55T, 65T, 68B, 70T, 70B, 72T, 83T, 88T, 89B	**Denise Tackett**
38B, 39T, 39B, 42T, 45B, 46B, 51T, 51B, 79M, 80T, 88B, 91T, 91B	**Shoo-Yin Lim**
21B	**Manfred Gottschalk/Apa Photo**
15	**Department of Information and Broadcasting, Malé**
35B	**Apa Photo/Superstock**
Senior Desktop Operator	**Suriyani Ahmad**
Handwriting	**V. Barl**
Cover Design	**Klaus Geisler**
Cartography	**Berndtson & Berndtson**

Index

INSIGHT *pocket* GUIDES

· ·
United States: Houghton Mifflin Company, Boston MA 02108
Tel: (800) 2253362 Fax: (800) 4589501

Canada: Thomas Allen & Son, 390 Steelcase Road East
Markham, Ontario L3R 1G2
Tel: (416) 4759126 Fax: (416) 4756747

Great Britain: GeoCenter UK, Hampshire RG22 4BJ
Tel: (256) 817987 Fax: (256) 817988

Worldwide: Höfer Communications Singapore 2262
Tel: (65) 8612755 Fax: (65) 8616438

❝ I was first drawn to the Insight Guides by the excellent "Nepal" volume. I can think of no book which so effectively captures the essence of a country. Out of these pages leaped the Nepal I know – the captivating charm of a people and their culture. I've since discovered and enjoyed the entire Insight Guide Series. Each volume deals with a country or city in the same sensitive depth, which is nowhere more evident than in the superb photography. ❞

Sir Edmund Hillary

INSIGHT GUIDES

COLORSET NUMBERS

You'll find the colorset number on the spine of each Insight Guide.